THE LAMPBLACK BLUE OF MEMORY

MY MOTHER ECHOES

SARAH ADLEMAN

TOLSUN BOOKS

TOLLESON, ARIZONA & LAS VEGAS, NEVADA

The Lampblack Blue of Memory: My Mother Echoes

Copyright © 2019 by Sarah Adleman. All rights reserved. Printed in the United States of America. First Edition. For more information, contact Tolsun Books at tolsunbooks@gmail.com.

Edited by Brandi Pischke

No part of this book may be used or reproduced in any manner whatsoever without the prior written permission of the copyright holder except for brief quotations in critical articles or reviews.

The prose poem "Remember the Casseroles" first appeared in Kindred Magazine. A version appears in these pages.

Cover art by Dr. Debbie Pischke based on "Olfactory Bulb Neuronal Circuit." Camillo Golgi. 1875.

Set in Garamond, 11pt font and Courier, 9pt font.
Design by David Pischke

ISBN 978-1-948800-23-5

Published by Tolsun Books, LLC
Tolleson, Arizona & Las Vegas, Nevada
www.tolsunbooks.com

For Max, Ender, and Rumi.

AN INSUFFICIENCY OF JACKSON SQUARE

One Tuesday you give me
Jackson Square.

Two arms, a portfolio
and a shopping bag from Maison Blanche
cannot hold it all.

I stack surplus pieces in
your studio.

They melt.
You paint my portrait green
Jackson Square light.

I take the summer
inside me for a while.

(1969)

PROLOGUE

I recently bought a 1969 Honda CT70 motorbike. After traveling around Asia for a stint, I became infatuated with the ease women drove the streets, often carrying children in school uniforms with backpacks or plastic bags of groceries that billowed in the wind of movement. There was a freedom they embodied, wrapped in ability and control. I returned home with a photo of me sitting on a parked bike in front of a laundromat in Luang Prabang. The bike is painted matte kelly green. There are no decals or emblems painted to indicate where the bike originated, just the curvature of the steel body.

I used this photograph to internet scour and decided the bike I was searching for was the Honda CT70. It was born in 1961 out of a child's amusement park ride in Tokyo. The mini motorcycles were attached to a metal ring that allowed the riders to safely sit while they spun in circles for a few minutes. By 1969, Honda had designed a larger bike meant for trails and countryside and began to export to the United States. The exhaust pipes on the CT70s are raised making it less burdensome to traverse water.

I found the bike, candy sapphire blue, during a spring dust

storm. It sat outside of The Red Door Vintage Shop in El Paso, Texas parked beside a rack of polyester shirts and brassieres. I'd been dreaming of my own Zen experience of disassembling the old body and laying each part in numbered rows and columns, cleaned by hand, fixed. I wanted to know how each part was connected and why each part was necessary.

The bike has a four-stroke engine powered by internal combustion.

FIRST STROKE: INTAKE

The piston begins within the cylinder at top dead center. It descends from the top to the bottom. The volume within increases. Fuel and air combine and are forced by natural pressure—greater if it's by additional force—into the cylinder through the intake port.

My brothers and I believed our father was Crocodile Dundee when we were young. As a family we'd drive to our Aunt and Uncle's house and while the adults sat outside drinking margaritas, we'd lie on the mauve carpet inside and watch *Crocodile Dundee*. Our father would pass through the living room and he'd stop to reminisce about life in the bush, his blonde hair and tan body resonant to the man on screen. We believed, like kids at the tail end of believing in Santa Claus, our father could wrestle a crocodile, that he could, if his life depended on it, learn to breathe under water.

He ran marathons when we were growing up. Consequently, we spent many Saturdays at Fun Runs cheering him on. Marathon mornings we'd wake-up to the theme song of *Chariots of Fire* on repeat blaring through the house. We'd travel to the different mile markers waiting for our father and then the go-ahead from our mother to run beside him briefly. At the finish line, we'd crowd into the fence and cheer with the hundreds of others who were, in our minds, all cheering for him.

He once rode a 2-speed bicycle he bought at a garage sale for $30 from Houston to Austin in the annual MS150 race. Typically people train for months, set-up rollers in their living room, spend whole weekends preparing for the two days of riding in the Texas hill country. Not him. He was invited to ride, found a bike, and completed the challenge. He spent his life preparing by never backing down from a challenge. He took on the loss of his wife by trying to outmatch grief's hurt. For each thump grief initiated, he stood with his arms open sucking it in, allowing it to become all he knew.

The CT70 sat in my backyard for nine months. It was missing an air filter so I didn't ride it for fear of ruining the engine. The front brakes didn't work. Both the headlight and taillight were burnt out and the tires were rotten. I quickly discovered that I would need more than a wrench and a screwdriver to disassemble and properly reassemble this machine. I searched for a mechanic who might be interested in letting me use their space and their knowledge of all things mechanical while I brought the bike back to life. Eventually my desire to ride the bike surpassed my desire of the imagined Zen experience. I found Lorenzo, a retired man in his late seventies who dressed in ostrich skin boots, Wranglers, and button down shirts on Tuesdays—even when it's ninety-five degrees outside. I have trouble understanding him, his speech garbled in an accent and a mouth that barely opens. But I trust he knows what he's doing. I just want to ride the bike. I give him the keys and we shake hands. No paperwork. No upfront payment. That's not what this is about.

SECOND STROKE: COMPRESSION

The intake and exhaust valves close. The piston returns to the top of the cylinder compressing the fuel and air it has sucked into the cylinder head.

When I was sixteen my father taught me how to change a tire in front of our house. He explained how to use a jack, the proper way to loosen and subsequently tighten the lug nuts, and the importance of not driving over 50mph on a spare. I remember him standing over me while I sat on the concrete curb and used all of my arm strength to loosen the flat tire from the wheel well.

The main reason one doesn't want to drive on a spare for an extended period of time is because the tire has little to no tread. The difference in size between it and the other three tires causes the spare to spin faster when the vehicle is in motion. Even if one doesn't drive over 50mph, after seventy miles the lubricating grease on the gears and clutch plates wear down from the imbalance causing a slew of consequential effects. *One can only drive on a spare for so long,* he said. *They make us vulnerable.*

He went years without truly laughing. My two brothers and I became therapists, nutritionists, friends, and parents. Never again would we just be children. For a long time I said, *I lost a parent, but he lost his life love.* This is not better or worse, it is simply the way it is. We tried. When we realized he wasn't backing down from the hurt, when he embodied the victim, we tried harder. When he curled up in the grass where her body was found, we tried to coax him back to reality.

There is a tipping point when perseverance, the quality of determination and grit, becomes perseverance, a stubborn insistence. My brothers and I all ran our first marathon together simply so our father would run again. There was no way he would let his three children run without him. The four of us signed up for the Marine Corps Marathon in Washington, D.C. and trained individually around the country. The year we ran, the rule was, if a runner makes it to the 14th Street Bridge before the straggler bus, then he or she can take as long as they need to finish the remaining five miles. The cramps were gripping my father's legs when he heard the bus behind him, the bridge insight. He maneuvered his body, carrying fifty extra pounds of grief and fat, the bus approaching, the volunteer at the bridge cheering him forward. He was the last one they allowed on the bridge to finish the race. When he crossed the finish line, between the two marines standing at attention, just past the cast-bronze soldiers lifting the American flag, and filed into one of the empty cues to receive his medal, the announcer was gone. The crowds of other runners and volunteers and spectators had long since left. Even his children had gathered out-of-sight waiting for him to catch-up.

Lorenzo called me periodically with updates and permission to replace different parts and approval of costs. I understand him less on the phone than in person and give the okay to everything he recommends. I repeat "whatever you think" and "let's get it right" and "thank you so much for your help" often throughout each of our conversations. One day he calls and says, "It's ready."

THIRD STROKE: POWER

This is the start of the second revolution in the cycle. The piston is at top dead center. The compressed fuel-air mixture ignites from a spark plug. The pressure from the combustion forces the piston back down to bottom dead center.

Standing to the side of the bike, his hands on both handlebars, Lorenzo steps down on the kick-starter with his black ostrich boot. The engine grumbles. I strain to understand what he is saying, repeating back what I hear. We kneel on either side of the engine. He runs his finger along the brake line and shows me how to turn on the lights, how to control the throttle, though this last piece of information is lost to the garble and noise of the engine. We load the bike into the back of my truck. Lorenzo and his son work together to secure the bike to the bed--years of knowledge and experience feed an old climbing rope through his hands and around the tires and handlebars and steel body. I stand in the bed of the ruck trying to help, trying not to be in the way. not knowing how to express my gratitude I tell him the bike has good juju because of him. He chuckles, then turns towards his house, his Wranglers just touching the top of his boots.

My mother taped sheets of paper that said *Choose Joy* all over the house—on bathroom mirrors, closet doors, inside kitchen cabinets—we grew up with this constant reminder to choose. Nobody took them down after she was gone. The adhesive on the tape slowly dried and the papers fell— behind the toilet, to the ground, on dinner plates. In geometry there is a figure called Gabriel's Horn, named after the archangel. It has infinite surface area but finite volume. Love is like this. Infinite in its nature, but contained within the capacity of our humanness—by the confines of the mind. We each have a horn and breath to blow our love sounds.

Sometimes, we have to blow hard enough for others who are out of breath. Sometimes, we sound to the heavens noises from inside, cacophonous, threatening deaf ears listen.

Sometimes, we touch our lips to the divine and it is enough.

FOURTH STROKE: EXHAUST

The piston once again returns to top dead center. The exhaust valve opens and expels the spent fuel-air.

The day I returned home with the bike I unloaded her into the backyard and tried to start the engine like Lorenzo did, but couldn't. I stepped my legs onto either side of the bike and held onto the handlebars. With force fueled by the fear of failure I stepped down with power and the engine grumbled.

I sat on the bike and spent a minute trying to remember how to put her into gear. And then in less than ten seconds crashed into the back of the house when I couldn't remember how to brake. The engine cut off, my right shin and foot throbbed from being slammed into the base of a nearby chair. I sat stunned, scared, wanting to cry. I tried to understand why the action for acceleration, pulling one's shoulders back and tightening the grip on the handle bars, is the same action of the body's natural reaction to stop movement.

The next day I pulled the bike into the middle of my back-yard and propped open the kickstand. After watching You-Tube videos on the best way to remove rust from chrome and steel, I proceeded with confidence. Three types of steel wool lay on the table, along with a roll of paper tow-els, and the set of rearview mirrors I intended to install. I opened an IPA and began the process. It's exhilarating to watch the rust clean back to silver. I scrubbed for hours my world reduced down to the square millimeters in front of me. The steel wool splintered and punctured my skin leaving blood pricks that lasted for weeks. My forearms cramped. The rust chipped away into thousands of specks and fell to filth on my crossed legs. Each spec of iron ag-gregate is different, like a snowflake that has fallen through the Earth's atmosphere collecting its different angles as it falls through differing temperatures, forged into unique-ness. I lean down to my ankles and blow. The specks don't move—they will remain until I clean my own filthy body.

*

For a long time my father refused to give up, let go, ac-knowledge his decision to grip the gates of Hell. My brothers and I tried to carry him—lift his heavy body, and hoist him onto our shoulders. When he fought, we let go. No matter how much we beckoned from flower-covered hills, we couldn't make him move. Occasionally, I join him at the gates and hold his hand, knowing he is being forged and perhaps one day he may choose to return to top dead center for another revolution.

Out beyond ideas of wrongdoing and rightdoing,
there is a field. I'll meet you there.
When the soul lies down in that grass,
the world is too full to talk about.
Ideas, language, even the phrase
"each other" doesn't make any sense.

~Mevlana Jelaluddin Rumi

The black soot that remains after coal burns is called lamp-black, or channel black. It is what's left after incomplete combustion. It is used to make ink, paint, or products like the soles of shoes or rubber tires. It is one of the first pigments known to man found in ancient cave art, and today, found in factories, fueled into production. Past ash creations become carbon copies of what was into what is, returning the cycle back once more.

Eric Kandel, Nobel Prize Laureate in medicine for his work on learning and memory, correlates the communication of neurons to that of one person whispering into the ear of another.

In three parts:

the lips that speak   the space between   the ears that hear

Quietly the sky bleeds red the open gash of Autumn sunset.

Where does memory go when all have died
who once gave the past a life?

As bales of fog line the docks, rain
whispers secrets. I am not alone.

I've written the letter. It took four months, though I suppose really it took eighteen years. A letter that began slow, as most letters written towards ourselves do. The letter, sealed inside of an envelope and addressed to a place I gathered was real, though I found it on the internet, was handed over to the young girl working behind the counter, metered, and sent to a man whose reality I'd just begun to realize.

It would have been enough to simply write the words. The words gathered out of the sludge of me, hidden beneath rocks unturned, crevices forgotten, echoes lost. It would have been enough to haul the words out, lay them to dry, clues of crumpled salt and grit—a map to the place I didn't know I was looking for. It would have been enough. But after I pieced them together, wrote them into existence, the process was only sublimated to the surface, lacking in some-not-yet-known way.

I mailed the letter mid-morning on Tuesday, December 29th. It takes between two and seven days for delivery from here to there, minus the postal holiday of January 1st, setting the arrival time sometime between Thursday, December 31st and Friday, January 8th. Once delivered, all mail is opened and searched for contraband like razor blades, string, or prohibited material—written or visual. The Texas Department of Criminal Justice correspondence rules state all mail must be processed within two business days. It is possible, if the letter arrived the morning of Thursday, December 31st that it was vetted, approved, and delivered that afternoon, before the mailroom employees turned off the lights and left for the long holiday weekend.

It is more likely the letter was delivered the first week of January.

I don't actually think he will respond. And it's not his response I want. I simply want to know the cycle was completed. My words were heard. But I don't realize this just yet. I still think I'm looking for answers. I still feel like answers might bring sense.

The girl behind the counter can't meter something that doesn't exist yet, so I affix a stamp from home to a return envelope and stuff it inside. Stamps are considered contraband and my return envelope will be tossed when opened by the prison mailroom staff. If inmates don't have funds in their accounts to purchase stamps or envelopes, the state will provide up to five of each per month. More if the letters are of legal matters. I don't want to take anything of his. An envelope, a stamp—insignificant, but somehow magnanimous in the gesture. There is too much unsaid. Too much that will never be said. To take something of his he has willingly offered is, at the very least, an act of acknowledgement and at most a dialogue of forgiveness. Forgiveness requires letting go, and even though I feel my stomach drop when I pass the sealed envelope to the girl in front of me, I try to maintain as much control over the situation as possible by including a stamped return envelope.

I don't check the PO Box until Monday, January 25th. When I do there are three pieces of mail for the woman who had the address before me and a letter postmarked January 8th. It's not my handwriting, but his. It's not the stamp I sent, but rather a Forever stamp with fireworks bursting in red glare across an American Flag. I close the small metal box and turn the key. My legs are shaking. I can't get my eyes to focus. I can barely get my hands to clasp the thin white envelope, size $4^{1/8}$x $9^{1/2}$, the approved size inmates of the Texas Department of Criminal Justice are allowed to mail.

On the street I am acutely aware of the freedom I have. Of the freedom everyone around me has, the couples sharing coffee, the woman behind me who says she likes the wine colored gloves in the window, the group of baggy panted teenagers who've gathered with a boombox on the corner of 16th and Lawrence. The distance between everyone on the outside and everyone on the inside, between him and the rest of humanity has never felt greater, nor more imagined. My breath has become metered. Controlled. This is when it begins to snow. Light at first, hardly noticeable. But soon, gradually, as I make my way back home, the sky and the ground turn white, covering everything. Covering all that I know, all that I have ever known, in silence.

There are only two choices in a neuron: to fire or not to fire. This firing, or not firing, results in our actions: to speak or to remain silent, to move or to stay still. Each of our actions, the movement of one foot in front of the other or the muscles of the mouth opening, the tongue touching the teeth to form sound, each decision distills back to the neuron.

Beginning in the space of our mind, the neuron electrifies the message of intended action down the length of its axon to the synaptic terminal. Here, there is space. The synaptic cleft, like the space between one star and another or the space between your face and the face of another, is where the message changes from electrical to chemical. Where the message, like words being spoken, changes from the thoughts in our heads to the sounds that transverse across and enter the ears listening. If the ears hear the words they are computed back into thought. Or in the case of a neuron, back into electrical code and the process repeats. One neuron whispering into the ear of another. This pathway establishes our habits and thoughts, our perceptions and memory. The brain from where we live.

Sometimes we are aware of the words we will speak before they leave our mouths. Consciously thinking about what and how we will voice the thoughts inside our head. Which course of action we will pursue. Often, though, the words are of impulse—an instantaneous reaction to other words spoken around us, or to us. The mind cycling through the rolodex of memories and experiences, choosing a lightning quick path to proceed. The past, present in each moment, creates the space for how we move forward.

Remember when you straddled your bicycle at the top of the driveway? Your feet barely touched the concrete below. Your father, holding the seat behind you, tells you not to look back and not to stop pedaling. You can feel him steadying the sway as he pushes you down the long drive. *Don't stop*, he says, *Keep going.* And you do, down the drive, past the mailbox, and into the cul-de-sac ahead. This is when you realize he is no longer behind you. You don't look back. You watch the road slip beneath the tires and begin to balance into what feels like an act you've always known.

Your neurons connect as you pedal. This is where learning and memory reside. Not within the neuron, but as Eric Kandal writes, *in the connections it receives and makes with other cells in the neuronal circuit to which it belongs.* The train stops alongside the Mississippi River in Minneapolis and I'm reminded of crossing the New Bridge into Baton Rouge on visits to my mother's hometown. Those times we would pack into the Beretta or later, the Crown Victoria. My brothers and I vying for space the entire drive from the bayous of Houston to the swamps of Louisiana.

Grape bubble-yum, the plastic drum of generic cheese-puffs, the green *500 Jokes & Riddles* book tucked into the webbing on the back of the seat. It's not about nostalgia. The importance of these details comes from their foundational basis of memory, for the beginning of our story. (This story.) When neurons first lay down the tracks of our whys and hows.

Bayous pulse over the flat land of Houston like veins on a hand, like roots of a mangrove. When brothers Augustus and John Allen arrived at the headwaters of the Buffalo Bayou in the summer of 1836, shortly after Texas won independence from Mexico, they identified the land wild with Sicklepod flowers and Sweetgum trees and hundreds of waterways to be the future site for present-day Houston. They bought the 6,642 acres, previously granted to John Austin by Mexico, and began the process of connecting the booming city of Galveston to the new town of Houston. Gail Borden Jr., who'd made the first topographical map of Texas and who would later invent condensed milk, was hired to survey the land and lay out the streets that now comprise downtown. The Chamber of Commerce was established in 1840 and by 1853 the Buffalo Bayou, Brazos & Colorado Railroad connected Houston to the rest of the country that was undergoing rapid change fueled by the desire to connect. By the early 1900s Houston adopted the slogan, *Where Seventeen Railroads Meet the Sea.* Christian Wolmar, one of the world's principal railroad experts, writes, *without the railroads, the United States would not have become the United States.* We flourished with our new found ability to resource time.

Like most inventions, the train was a gradual evolution over time reinforced by society's desire to do more, have more, be more. The first reference of enabling a speedier passage of goods and people over land is the *Diolkos*

i lose the simplicity of grass. leaf-bright summers

(17)

which crossed the Isthmus of Corinth off of Greece's Ionian coast. The four-five mile stretch of land consisted of a limestone road with grooved tracks that guided large wooden flatbed cars between the Gulf of Corinth to the Saronic Gulf. This path allowed ships to be hoisted out of the water on one side, conveyed across the land on the wooden cars, then re-enter the water on the other side, thus avoiding the often treacherous journey around the Peloponnesian Peninsula. Historians gather this passage was in use from about 600 B.C. to 50 A.D. But even before *Diolkos,* wagon ways connected cities of people to trading posts or sacred places. Ruts cut into the stone of the earth allowed for the faster transportation of people and goods.

It wasn't until the seventeenth century, Denis Papin invented a working pressure cooker and lay the framework for the first steam engine. Using Papin's intention, Thomas Savery perfected the design and by 1698 the invention was being used to either pump water out of mines or supply water to large buildings. The design was still lacking though, and couldn't handle more powerful tasks. But in 1712, Thomas Newcomen built upon Papin's and Savery's ideas to invent the much more efficient and powerful atmospheric steam pump. And it was James Watt, who in 1764, while repairing a Newcomen engine in the shop he owned, took notice of how much steam was being wasted and invented the separate condenser in order to save the latent heat—the heat used to change the state of a substance— from solid to liquid, from liquid to gas. This was Watt's first invention and by many accounts the main attraction of the Industrial Revolution. The *Salamanca*, built in 1812, by Mathew Murray, was the first successful locomotive and ran between Middleton and Leeds in Britain. And finally in 1830, *Tom Thumb,* built by Peter Cooper became the first American made locomotive.

Prior to trains in America, were horse drawn carts with steel wheels that glided over steel rails. Mostly used in quarries and coal mines for hauling out the insides of the earth, the builders of America had their sights set on a series of canals to connect the cities of the East. A much more efficient way to transfer goods and people than the standard horse drawn trailer. With the development of the steam engine, however, everything changed. A stretch of rail could go in overnight and the speed at which a train could travel far outpaced the system of canals. By the 1850's the spirit of the railroad was establishing the body of America. From the industrial tycoons who funded the endeavors, to the laborers who laid and pounded rail after rail, the East connected to the West, the West to the East, and all of the places in between. As a brain functions in innovation and production when connected, this same framework propelled America forward.

Fueled by coal—carbon linked to hydrogen and oxygen, once living cells of plants and organic matter, pressurized.

of the towhee. my feet are planted as one who stands waiting.

Hidden under rocks inside the earth's body and cooked by her internal heat over thousands of years. Coal is created. Black lumps of energy to be burned. To heat the water and produce steam. To pump the pistons and create movement. To move the wheels forward.

The Allen brothers saw the economic importance of Houston's location on the Southern coast. Following the Hurricane of 1900 that killed more than 8,000 and decimated most of Galveston, construction on a fifty-two mile ship channel from the Gulf of Mexico to Houston commenced. When the channel opened in 1912, President Woodrow Wilson pressed a button from his office in Washington D.C. and a cannon shot out across the Southern waters to mark the start of what would become the nation's leading port in foreign tonnage. Houston was now connected to the rest of the country via the rails. The city joined the economic bustle of the 19th century and began to expand along the naturally occurring pathways of the bayous. Today there are over 2,500 miles of these waterways connecting through the city centers of Downtown, the Medical Center, the Museum District, and the Galleria. They pulse out into the suburbs and surrounding areas with banks of concrete and Sicklepod, along dirt paths flanked by tall grass where on any given day thousands are found walking or running, riding their bicycles, together or alone.

here among the mosses lightening will show my tendril feet climbing the dark oak.

In 1977 both my mother and father joined the one million others who moved to Houston during the decade. My father, after attending The University of Texas at Austin and then serving as an officer in the Navy for four years. He moved into a garage apartment in the Heights. My mother, after living at home while attending Louisiana State University and then completing her MFA in Theatre Arts at The University of Minnesota. She pulled Houston out of a hat of possible places to move and bought a small 2 bed/1 bath on a street that dead ends into the White Oak bayou. In the summer of 1978 they met at a party my father threw. He was making fresh strawberry daiquiris. She was on a blind date. Her date asked for his daiquiri to be seedless and my father acquiesced without debate, without criticism, he strained the fresh, red juice from the pulp. Unaware the path his life would take pivoted on this encounter. In one exchange my mother knew two things:

In night and intimate communion
when all else is faded off the edges
        of the world
in some other light
into some other place into China
or the highest place in the world
        Tibet
(which cannot be reached, by the way,
            through a hole
in the ground — a hole bears, no
        direction here)
when the darkness seeps around and ties
        our shadows together,
piecing the extracts of the day into
        union, soft and faceless,
ties the night that slowly takes the form
        of a woman's underbelly
and we can all return to our mates,
        our whores
or our "cradles endlessly rocking"

In night and intimate communion
when I can come to no sure consequence
nor do I have to
I feel my hands clutch full of the form

(22)

she wouldn't involve herself seriously
with someone who requested the
seeds of strawberries to be removed
at a house party, and she wanted to
better know the man who would treat
a stranger with open kindness, with no
judgement. My parents married less
than a year later and moved into her
house off of the White Oak Bayou.
My memories from this house are
two-dimensional, latent images printed
between sheets of mylar plastic and
sticky glue. The second bedroom
turned nursery decorated with the
half-domes of rainbows. Asleep, next
to my father on the orange and green
patchwork quilt that covered their bed.
My mother holding a platter of boiled
crabs, my father shirtless holding a
basket of fresh picked cucumbers from
the garden. Easter morning, wearing a
cotton white jumper holding lilies taller
than me. Another morning, drinking
from the hose in the backyard, beneath
the concrete birdbath.

of you,
follow the directions like a voyageur
    traces stars
to a sure destination
and the sheets become damp as night
    air through the shutters.

Night will not be shut. It will stay.
Night does not journey to Tibet.
You are as sure to me as a recurring dream
I will never fully realize
nor take to lodge with me
in my real life with eyelids sprung
our mouths busy digging separate holes
into New Tibets.
You will always be sure.
Each night.
Each separate celebration of communion
with shadows.
Actions become the love itself.

We have put between us time and space and other things we swore we would never mention.

or terminals; somehow we have earned the right to be divided. I do not count the time.

The snow grows thicker outside. At night I turn off all the lights inside and press my face against the cold glass. The train windows cast just enough light to see the snow piled darkness beyond, maybe a forest of trees or an open plain, or perhaps nothing. Just us, the tracks the only indicator of where we've been, that we were once here. For a moment, another set of rails runs alongside this moving body, two lines the exact distance necessary to carry the weight of this train. The snow is too thick to see the ties underneath. Laid on crushed stone and coal ash, connected by the rails above—the rails running alongside my window, a reflection of my path mirrored, until our tracks turn one direction and theirs turn the other. The tracks disappear into the darkness beyond the snow, the darkness beyond the snow covered ground.

We are all that move in a stand-still.
It is the other things that add the miles.

My brother Geoff was born in 1983 and the four of us moved soon after from the house on the White Oak bayou to a house on Bayou Vista. The house sat in the back of a neighborhood on a cul-de-sac. The gate in the backyard opened to the bayou and it was on this bayou, on a Sunday afternoon, at age seven, I learned to cartwheel. I set the worthy number of 500 and spent the afternoon cartwheeling up and down the bayou counting each time a revolution was completed, knowing each time it was one more than ever before. Like most things, the process is slow at first, standing with arms overhead, pausing for a moment, looking at the ground ahead, thinking about the action, initiating the movement. It becomes easier with each rotation. The body and brain begin to find rhythm, become familiar with the movement. When the sun starts to set, she calls from the gate at the bayou and I cartwheel off of the dirt path, through the backyard, and onto the street out front, around and around the cul-de-sac, the pavement pressing the loose gravel and the awareness of the uneven terrain into my hands. Each rotation rubs deeper into callous.

When learning is taking place, our neurons pulse serotonin at the synaptic terminal which releases glutamate and strengthens the synapse communicated. When a memory is stored long-term the intensity of the serotonin increases. This causes not only increased amounts of glutamate, but also growth of new synaptic connections. In order for this new growth to occur, the nucleus of the neuron becomes involved. It activates a protein that binds to our

She asked me to teach her how a cartwheel is thrown. I knew such things have to be

genes—the building code for our existence—two perfectly spaced lines spun into a double helix. This protein regulates which memories are stored by creating a threshold of sorts to ensure only important, life-serving experiences are learned. The more one activity is repeated, like tying a shoe or learning a language, the more protein is released and the stronger the synaptic connections become. The repetition necessary for long-term memory storage is bypassed during heightened emotion or life altering moments. In these cases, the protein is released so rapidly the memory is automatically stored into long-term.

Do not go into the water, she said and handed me the cardboard box. I held it tight with all the expectation of adventure ahead and turned towards the bayou. Again and again, down the grassy slope bumping over rocks, gripping the cardboard sides all the way down to the water. Each time, moving further down the bayou as if in an ocean tide. With the box under my arm I'd make the trek back to the top, brush the escaped hair from my ponytail out of my face, and begin again. Each time, the crowd cheering in my head grew louder and when the cardboard box hit a rock and tumbled me onto the banks and it joined the current of the bayou, I had no choice but to rescue the invaluable item. I took off my shoes and stepped into the water. I watched my feet step carefully onto the bottom of the bayou, silty and deceptively familiar. I watched until the water became murky and too deep to see the bottom.

lived into. "You'll find out how," I said, "on your own

I don't know what she saw first—her child soaked and frightened or the tracks of blood. I do know she wrapped me in a towel, sat me down on a wooden dining room chair, and put a mixing bowl filled with warm water at my feet. Her jaw clenched, she didn't say a word. The dirt and blood dissolved, turned the water the color of rust. She lifted my feet out of the water and held my legs steady. When she poured hydrogen peroxide over the gashes and they fizzed white I wanted to scream. Instead, I gripped the chair tighter, both of our faces drawn in silence.

Sensory stimulus leads to two types of changes in the nervous system. Excitability and Plasticity. Excitability generates one or more action potentials in a neuronal pathway. This causes a refractory period where the firing of the action potentials briefly raises the threshold for generating additional action potentials in those neurons. These are the moments we remember. When the pathways in our brains are heightened, altering themselves from outside stimuli, coding for future survival. However, learning and memory storage are not dependent on external stimuli. Rather, when two stimuli inside interact, then learning results. Plasticity is a functional transformation resulting in changed patterns, behaviors, and thought.

(It's turning your world upside down: hand over hand and heel over heel—and staying in balance.)

In the spring of 1989 my parents filed for bankruptcy. The four of us moved again, further out of the city into Northwest Houston where the floor plans repeated every fourth house. The bayou still wove its way around the neighborhood, this time on three sides like a moat. The fourth side was a giant concrete sound wall that buffered the endless whooshing of cars on Beltway 8. A dead-end. One way in and one way out—except for the bayou. After school, while our parents were still at work, we'd ride the school bus to the end of our street and let ourselves into the empty house. We'd get whatever packaged or frozen snack we wanted, bought in bulk from Sam's, and watch TV—*The Monkees, Fresh Prince, MTV*. And then got to work on being kids in the 90's: visit friends, walk the block, climb the tree at the end of the cul-de-sac. Sit on the concrete banks of the bayou, the "Edge," we called it. The Edge of where our neighborhood ended and others began. The edge of perceived knowledge and innocent longing. I don't remember if this boundary was dictated by our parents or a self-imposed seat perched on the edge of our kingdom, the bayou flowing by below.

Zach was born a year after we moved and our parents sang *and tell me everything will be alright* as a proclamation and a prayer. The next seven years filled with memories: school talent shows and Boy Scout dinners, summers in daycare, summers in camps, summers in school. Friday nights at Two Amigos, returning home from seeing *Ghostbusters* and singing the theme song together as we all trailed off to bed. Waking to the *Chariots of Fire* theme song being blared from the stereo over the eight years our father and the one year our mother ran the Houston Marathon. First crushes, first kisses, sneaking out of bedroom windows, hiding friends in closets, learning to drive, testing limits, passing from children into the questioning, challenging years of adolescence. Over these years our parents spent most evenings in the backyard watching the sunset. After work, after running together on the bayou, they sat while the day faded into night. It didn't matter that the neighbor's house and fence blocked any real view of the actual sunset—you could feel it, the time of day when transition is palpable in light and color and air. This is when they stopped. Perhaps often just to touch the base of the other in the moments between full time jobs, three children, and trying to maintain their own individual footing.

I would walk on water, or at least try for you.
Sometimes it is hard enough to keep stable on the ground.

We do a lot of dirt walking
to reach the levee, then stop
still unsure of gravity.

The middle of America is sparse in the winter. Bare trees reveal undergrowth and the fallen dead. Broken branches tangle into what could be kindling. But there is too much snow. The woods give way to expanses of open white. Fields now barren. The rivers too are thick and slow—the atoms heavier: weighted by the new density. I am endlessly tired. Often I close my eyes and what feels like days pass. Often I close my eyes for days and when I open them again, the white sky still touches the earth, the empty trees still pass by, no leaves, just the base of form.

What if once, for instance, we start walking the other way—
say like on our elbows with feet planted into sky?
Nothing's sure but gravity.

Somewhere there must be buoyancy.
It isn't a question of sinking.
The answer is over water.

The earliest recorded death penalty laws date back to around 1760 B.C. written by King Hammurabi of Babylon. On concrete tablets he wrote his code. The death sentence was prescribed for a number of crimes, similar to a number of other codes in existence: the Jewish Torah, the Christian Old Testament, ancient Athenian law. When someone was put to death during these times it was a public spectacle and meant to be painful and slow. Ways included stoning, being burned at the stake, and even being trampled by a heard of elephants.

In Britain, under Henry VIII's thirty-seven year rule, it's estimated that 72,000 people were executed. In addition to the standards of being burned, hung, or beheaded, being boiled or drawn and quartered were also common practices. The nineteenth century Italian Minister Pelegrino Rossi wrote these punishments were *the poetry of Dante put into laws.*

ABANDON ALL HOPE YE WHO ENTER HERE.

The first recorded capital punishment in America took place in the Virginia Colony of Jamestown in 1608 for treason. Four years later the Governor of Virginia implemented the *Divine, Moral, and Martial Laws* for his constituents. Crimes punishable by death included killing chickens and stealing grapes. And in the colony of New York offenses such as denying the true God warranted death.

At my next rising you will not come with the lure of morning.

By the 1700's works from different writers like Voltaire and Cesare Beccaria began to question the standard practice of capital punishment and even began to theorize against it. Thomas Jefferson, William Bradford, Benjamin Rush, and Benjamin Franklin all worked to rein in the scope of crimes punishable by death arguing degrees of culpability. Over time, the general masses began to also see the gruesome forms of death as cruel towards their fellow man, even if that fellow man had broken a commitment to society. Death as punishment began to move towards being as painless as possible. Thus, hanging and the guillotine took stage—still as public spectacle. And although the severing of someone's head from their body is gruesome, it was fast and therefore seen as more compassionate. Plus, it was thought if society witnessed the act of someone being killed for a known crime it would reinforce law abiding tendencies. Foucault writes of these times, the system sought *not to punish less, but to punish better; to punish with an attenuated severity perhaps, but in order to punish with more universality and necessity; to insert the power to punish more deeply into the social body.* The first state to move executions out of a public venue and into a correctional facility behind walls was Pennsylvania in 1834. And in 1846, Michigan was the first state to abolish the death penalty completely. Other states followed and by the end of the 19th century, countries around the world were all coming to the same conclusion. However, this was simply a fractal effect and many other states in America and other countries around the world continued to deepen their beliefs in capital punishment.

I give your jacket to a farmer whose son is sixteen and cold.

Hanging was the main means of execution in America through the 19th century. The first electric chair was built in New York in 1888 and executed the first prisoner in 1890. The state of Texas authorized the use of the electric chair in 1923 and on February 8, 1924 executed the first Texas inmate. Four more were executed by electrocution that same day. The same year, after a failed attempt to pump cyanide gas into an inmate's cell while he slept, the State of Nevada built the first gas chamber to be used in the United States.

The peak of executions in America was between 1920-1940. During the 1930's, an average of 167 people a year were put to death. Compare this to the statistics of the second highest year: ninety-eight people in 1999. The 1930's were also arguably one of the worst economic periods of our country. On January 29, 1919, Congress signed into law the 18th Amendment banning the production, transportation, and sale of alcohol which went into effect a year later. The law caused thousands of Americans to lose their jobs when businesses associated with alcohol became illegal. Breweries, distilleries, saloons, even restaurants were forced to shut down. It's estimated that during the twelve year ban America governed the 18th Amendment, eleven billion dollars in tax revenue was lost and about $300 million was spent trying to enforce the law. Then, on October 29, 1929 the stock market crashed. And further west, in the American Plains, the worst drought in recorded history made it impossible for seeds to take root,

His sugar-cane wagon is piled with all of me that belonged to you.

for crops to grow. The Great Depression began. In a presidential radio address given on October 18, 1931, President Herbert Hoover argued that what was facing America was the question of *human relations, which reaches to the very depths of organized society and to the very depths of human conscience.* He argued that American life was built on the responsibility each of us has to our fellow man and the plight America was facing was from *failure to observe these primary yet inexorable laws of human relationship.* President Hoover was unseated by the election of Franklin D. Roosevelt in 1932 who ran on the platform to end prohibition. It's said he celebrated his win with a dirty martini and over the course of the next eight years more people were put to death than any other time in American history.

However, post-World War II between 1950-1970, support of the Death Penalty in America and other countries came to an all time low. Perhaps the world had witnessed enough killing. Appeals reached an all time high and the average length of stay for someone on Death Row increased from six months to two years.

In 1958, the Supreme Court interpreted what the forefathers meant by *cruel and unusual punishment* in the trial of Trop v. Dulles, a citizenship case. Chief Justice Warren concluded *the basic concept underlying the Eighth Amendment is noth-*

I will become tomorrow a hill rising in Louisiana, falling in Mississippi

ing less than the dignity of man. While the state has the power to punish, the Amendment stands to assure that this power be exercised within the limits of civilized standards. He goes on to speak the words that are often quoted in opposition to the Death Penalty, *The Amendment must draw its meaning from the evolving standards of decency that mark the progress of a maturing society.* Fourteen years later, in 1972, the court is asked to decide if the death penalty violates the Eighth Amendment. In a five-four vote and over 200 pages of dissents and concurrences the court rules the current application of the Death Penalty to be in violation of the Eighth Amendment. In his concurring statements, Mr. Justice Brennen writes, *Death is truly an awesome punishment. The calculated killing of a human being by the State involves, by its very nature, a denial of the executed person's humanity.*

He concludes further, *In the United States, as in other nations of the western world, the struggle about this punishment has been one between ancient and deeply rooted beliefs in retribution, atonement or vengeance on the one hand, and, on the other, beliefs in the personal value and dignity of the common man that were born of the democratic movement of the eighteenth century, as well as beliefs in the scientific approach to an understanding of the motive forces of human conduct, which are the result of the growth of the sciences of behavior during the nineteenth and twentieth centuries.*

with no end. The sparrow hawk will turn dark circles over stubble fields.

(43)

Mr. Justice Blackmun dissented with his opinion that the Death Penalty *violates childhood's training and life's experiences, and is not compatible with the philosophical convictions I have been able to develop. It is antagonistic to any sense of "reverence for life."* *... I fear the Court has overstepped. It has sought and has achieved an end.* It is this moral conflict and question of degrees of culpability that lead to the nine year moratorium on all executions. Over 600 sentences were moved from Death to Life. Then, in 1976, the Supreme Court ruled that State assigned capital punishments may continue and a man in Utah is executed by firing squad. The corneas from his eyes were saved and donated for a transplant giving the gift of sight to another.

Today, there are five legal methods of execution in the United States. Lethal Injection. Electrocution. Gas Chamber. Hanging. Firing Squad.

The state you're prosecuted in determines the eventual method in which you will die. Although lethal injection is the primary method for the thirty-three states in which the Death Penalty is a path, Tennessee would impose the electric chair if the lethal drugs were unattainable. Oklahoma, the gas chamber. Utah, the firing squad.

But most likely it will be lethal injection—bound to a gurney. Imagine: someone attaches heart monitors to your chest and you (and everyone else in the room) can hear the beep, beep, beep of the beat inside. Another someone (maybe the same someone) will then insert two needles into your veins. This person is not medically trained. So, be wary if they miss the vein and the drug goes into the muscle. There will be intense pain. They may have trouble finding a good vein. You will lie on the gurney, strapped down, while you are pricked again and again, your loved ones (maybe others you don't recognize) wait behind a concrete wall, thick glass window, curtain drawn, until the needle connects to the flow of your blood. The saline solution is started. The warden signals for the curtain to rise. Do you look? Do you look over to your children, your wife, to the faces you don't immediately recognize? They are looking at you. It's your last chance to look. Sodium thiopental will start to flow through your veins and this is the last memory you will have before falling asleep. Pavulon will be injected next. Your muscles will become paralyzed and then you will stop breathing. And finally, potassium chloride will stop the beating of your heart. Death by overdose. Death by respiratory and cardiac arrest. But you'll be unconscious. You won't feel a thing.

My mother kept a prayer garden in the backyard. Each morning before dawn, before the light ushered in the demands of day, she woke and sat next to the concrete birdbath carried from house to house to house, and the flowers planted and pruned each season. Roses, violas, butterfly weed. She didn't wear slippers or shoes, just barefoot, skin to concrete, cool and damp in the early Houston hours. The morning after she didn't come home I find a baby sparrow in the garden next to the birdbath, under the pine tree. If I can nurse the bird back to health my mother will be OK. I make a home for the bird in a shoebox, cut grapes for it to eat, and keep it on my bedside table for two nights.

Daniel Kahneman, Nobel Prize winner in Economics for his work with Amos Tversky on decision making, discusses the natural human tendency to find causality in the world: *a large event is supposed to have consequences, and consequences need causes to explain them.* Somehow causes bring meaning. If we can find causes or intentions then it helps to understand the place from where the effect was born.

In 1839, the anatomist Mattias Jakob Schleiden and Theodor Schwann formulated the now ubiquitously accepted fact of cell theory. The theory is composed of three basic precepts: First, all living organisms are made of cells (I am you and you are me). Second, the cell is the basic unit of life (Distilled to form, we are the same). Third, all cells are generated by other pre-existing living cells (Those before to those after).

i. I am new: an hour comes and opens me into the dark like a stiff, knotted bud of myrtle

Just a year earlier the first telegram in the United States was sent across two miles of wire in New Jersey. Congress saw the potential for this new form of communication and allocated $30,000 to Samuel Morse. A line was laid from the old Supreme Court chamber in Washington D.C. to the Mt. Clare Train Depot in Baltimore. On May 24, 1844, while Congress watched, Morse used his code of dashes and dots to send a message to Alfred Vail in Baltimore. Vail received the message, decoded it, and sent it back to the Capitol chamber waiting in silence. Morse read aloud, *What hath God wrought?* The message, suggested by Annie Ellsworth, the daughter of a friend of Morse, is taken from Numbers 23:23. The International Standard Version is the only translation that poses *What hath God wrought* as a question. The King James uses an exclamation mark and the Douay- Rheims a period. The Holman Christian Standard reads *What great things God has done!* and the International Standard translates the verse as, *What has God accomplished?*

ii I only trace my mapping by the slender branches of elm

The telegraph lines were installed across the country next to the railroads. And 150 years later fiber optic cables for high speed internet are laid along the same routes. America is connected by lines—rail lines, telegraph lines, telephone lines, internet lines—all drawn across for communication. All for intention of connection, to be more. Railroad historian and photographer, Lucius Beebe is quoted as saying, *It is no accident of circumstance that the most beautiful devisings and artifacts of American record have all been associated with motion and movement, the transport of people and things going somewhere else.* The transport of ideas and thoughts sent from one location to another.

I smell her in random places. It happens more in the first years after, in gas stations or on the streets of foreign cities. But mostly in grocery stores. It's her perfume. I follow the unsuspecting women up and down the aisles, stopping when they stop, moving when they move. Following like I also need apples and milk. Silently inhaling as if I might be able to breathe her into existence from the place she disappeared. Once, I asked a woman in front of me what perfume she was wearing. She looked up and answered like I knew she would, *Elixer.*

That's what my mom wore, I said.

my passing has not come

Memories are stored in the cerebral cortex—the outer layer of the brain, composed of gray matter, crumpled in on itself like a newspaper—where they are originally recorded. The memory of the last time I saw my mother is stored in the occipital lobe of my brain. She is standing in the living room, just home from work. I'm standing by the front door in running clothes on my way to the first cross-country practice of the season. It's a week before my senior year in high school. I'm frustrated at the perceived constraints of my life. I want to pierce a second hole in my ears and need parental approval because I am still sixteen. I'd watched my friend's brother numb his ear with ice and press a sewing needle through the lobe. Watched the fresh blood ooze down his neck. I wanted it to be fast—relatively painless. *Not today* she says. It was a Tuesday. Deciding my silence would serve as communication for my frustration, I turn to leave. *Sarah,* she calls to me from the doorway. I remember her saying *I love you.* But it could've been *I'll see you later.* I do remember looking back. Her smile. I want to remember I said *I love you too,* but in reality I think I just nodded. I do know I didn't walk across the living room. I didn't touch her, feel her arms, or touch her face. I will replay this moment in my mind forever. We are not quite frozen, we are breathing. Our eyes are blinking. One terminal emanating towards the other.

I've often wondered what his intention was the evening he threw his leg over the bicycle and started pedaling. What caused him to leave his house? Where was he headed? To the store to buy cigarettes (did he smoke?) or milk (for his children)? Or was it an unmediated impulsive action. A part of me wants him to have set out with the intention of: knowing she (women) ran on the bayou in the evening (sometimes alone). This, of course, leaves space for intervention—as thoughts exist in our mind, so does the potential to change them. To roll them over in consciousness, bathe them in perspective, before the action potential is fired.

Retroactively eternal—cause & effect. The snake eating its tail. David Hume argues there are only three principles of connection between different ideas: *resemblance, contiguity in time or place, and cause or effect.* Out of connection, our brains birth meaning. It feels wrong to find meaning in death. But it feels hopeless to find none.

The sun set while I ran the streets around my high school during practice. While she ran on the bayou behind our house. While my father watched the sky from the backyard—vivid orange and lavender lighting into formations. He was waiting for her to return when I got home. He waited until the sky turned dark and the cicadas moved to silence.

iii I disturb the air like a moth, like wings crawling wetly from one womb into another

Every time we recall an event we bring it back into consciousness. Restoring. But each time we recall, we resave
with input from the current moment. If the memory is recalled enough the event will become distorted, magnified,
polished. Our memories fall into two different categories:
implicit and explicit. Implicit memory is not recalled consciously, rather it is responsible for those motor and per-
ceptual skills that become second nature. Like running or
riding a bicycle. Explicit memory is what makes it possible
to simultaneously be in the present and the past and the
future. Our memory stores the nouns of our existence
from which our thoughts are drawn, to be inside of once
again, to relive. The physical body responds with the heart
beating faster, our breath catching, the stomach clenching
into a sharp pit. Or a deep breath, a release. With PTSD,
the pathway of a memory in heightened emotional stress
becomes hardwired into survival. Some soldiers who have
returned from combat with crippling PTSD have moved
through the hard work of rewiring these pathways. With
the work of re-remembering the event or re-visiting the
memory and armed with the tools of conscious knowledge, I've watched individuals re-circuit the traumatic
pathway away from fear and anger and into a place of stillness. It is something only they can do—with the intent of
moving through the space they found themselves stuck in,
re-living. No pill or external physical manipulation. The
work of the mind is ultimately internal. We are each the
conductors of our existence.

iv I respond to a form barking across the dark yard

I remember the helicopters and the reporters. The police. I remember the doorbell on the third day. I remember my friend's father standing at the threshold of the neighbor's house. Telling me to come home. I remember asking him while we walked if everything was ok. I remember him looking down at the ground and saying *not exactly, no.* I remember walking into the living room filled with family friends all silent. Being escorted into my bedroom. My brothers and father waiting. The thin quilted bed. I remember sitting between my brothers. My father kneeling on the ground in front of us. And here is where time freezes. Where we become stone statues replicated by preserved circumstance, like a display in the museum of mind. I lift the velvet rope and walk over to my father, his head lowered about to speak the words that will forever change our lives. I stand beside him and touch his head. Cup his ears from the scream that will leave us deaf for years.

Hold me heavy against a spring dusk.

Spin me long as silver thread. The circles of time we spend are bordered in silver and strong.

If this train were to flip, would I survive? If say we derailed, slid down the frozen bank and tumbled across the plains, would I ricochet inside my tiny compartment — against the glass and blue carpet walls and plastic bedside table. Would I be able to grip the seatbelt harness above me or maybe wrap an arm into the thick ribbed curtains while the metal train car crashed and sparked across the earth? I don't think I sleep, but when I wake the carpet burns across my face and forearms scathe. Was it not a dream? I lay in bed, still—watching the blue curtains sway and rattle from the tracks underneath.

The song of a cardinal pauses.

Crickets linger in the thought of a past afternoon. We simmer soft along a line of shadows.

The Love comes gently, pushing in everwidening circles
the echoes from around the core.

I bury the bird in the garden. Fold her wings in close to her body and use a paper towel like a shroud. With a hand trowel, I dig a hole beneath the pine tree, next to the concrete birdbath. It's Jewish tradition to place stones on graves, though this isn't why at sixteen I place stones on the bird's grave. It's an act of acknowledgement that under the earth lies a once living being. Nobody quite knows where the Jewish tradition stems from, but it became a mitzvah, a commandment. If you are walking from one town to another and pass by a cairn of stones, the mitzvah commands you stop. Pay homage, stack more stones. Rabbi Goldie Milgram makes an argument for stone to be a metaphor for God. The Ten Commandments were carved from stone. Moses beat the stone he was sitting on when his sister Miriam dies. Stoning was a form of capital punishment and stones were used to cover dead bodies as they lay on the earth. Decomposed cells returning to the form of the beginning.

In 2008, two art kits thought to be around 100,000 years old were discovered by a team of researchers in a South African cave. The kits included natural pigments like ochre and charcoal as well as grindstones, abalone shells, and bone. The researchers deduced that the pigment was ground into a fine powder and then mixed and heated with other crushed stones or bone in the abalone shells along with liquid of some sort. Perhaps blood or urine or animal fat. Artificial holes in the cave walls indicate temporary scaffolding was used for high, hard to reach corners, deep inside, void of light. Torches are necessary to illuminate the ancient expressions held on the walls. Sometimes a

If I could stay here long enough I would become landscape.

natural formation inside the cave indicates the location of the drawings. And sometimes it's sound. Sometimes, it's the places in the cave where the echo changes. A call, a vibration out, ricocheting the passageways, the crevices, an echo back—listen. Find the place where the change happens and like memories in a mind, pictographs mark the cave walls.

The German chemist, August Wilhelm Hofmann, began his research career by studying the chemical constituents of coal tar, or lampblack. His work spurred hundreds of experiments and discoveries in chemistry. One of his students, William Henry Perkin, discovered the synthetic composition for the color mauve in 1856 in a London laboratory. The dye industry exploded. The once expensive and hard to cultivate natural colors such as indigo and sienna became affordable and available as synthetic pigments. It was because of these discoveries in the world of chemistry, Santiago Ramón y Cajal was able to bring a neuron to light. He used a combination of soaking preserved blocks of brain tissue in a silver nitrate solution and the synthetic dyes which darkened the nerve cells—from the dendrites to the axons. The technique, developed by Camillo Golgi, the Italian physician who would later share the Nobel Prize with Cajal, was labeled *the black reaction*. It was these inventions that led to Cajal's established Neuron Doctrine: the nervous system is made of individual cells that form connections between one another. This doctrine falls under the broader cell theory.

Political parties have long staked territory in issues concerning life and death, the beginnings and endings of our time as citizens. Oklahoma is second in executions performed since 1976 and in May 2016 tried to increase the distance between the two landmarks by passing a law making it a felony for a woman to have an abortion. Even if rape or incest were involved. The bill passed with no debate and all members of the Senate in support except for one, Senator Irvin Yen, Republican, the only medical doctor on the Senate, who called the bill *insane.*

Although politics in Texas are starting to change, the reputation for electing officials staunched in pro-life and pro-death penalty legislation remains one of the state's political foundations and reached a tipping point in the eighties and early nineties. Ann Richards partially won election as Governor of Texas in 1991 by running on a platform of rehabilitation for criminals. However, after appointing judges and parole board members who favored prosecution power, Texas rejected funding its school system with $750 million and instead approved $1 billion to build more prisons. When running for reelection in 1990, Mark White's campaign aired a commercial of the former Texas governor walking through a display of large photos of people executed during his term to show his toughness against crime. And the oil and gas tycoon, Clayton Williams, who unsuccessfully ran as the republican gubernatorial candidate against Ann Richards and may be more infamously remembered for saying of rape *if it's inevitable,*

Rocks would fit me in among themselves—a strange new fossil—but accepted through long-staying.

(63)

relax and enjoy it, claimed his proposed laws to expand the death penalty were *the way to make Texas great again*. And in New York, when the prison population was outgrowing its walls, Governor Mario Cuomo ignored voter's wishes to not build more prisons and instead pulled money out of the Urban Development Corporation meant for building housing for the poor, and added more space in prison than any other governor in New York history.

However, since 1998, the number of people incarcerated on Death Row across America has been declining. In 2000–3,593 people. In 2009–3,173 people. On April 1, 2015–3,002 people. On October 1, 2015–2,959 people. On July 10, 2016—2,905 people. On July 1, 2017—2,817 people. On July 1, 2018—2,738 people. The decline in numbers is the result of several factors. The main reason is six states have since abolished the death penalty. Four of the states transferred all of their death row inmates to life in prison and two of the states chose to abolish the law but did not make it retroactive. Thus, there are still twelve inmates in Connecticut and two in New Mexico waiting to be executed in a state where capital punishment no longer exists. Six additional states choose not to abolish the death penalty, but to add Life without Parole as an option for the juries.

There were 299 people between 2000-2013 who died on death row because of natural causes, suicide, or murder by another inmate. Compared to the 761 people who were executed. Exonerations due to innocence account for the release of 157 people since 1973. The occurrence of people being wrongfully committed has significantly decreased due in part to DNA testing.

~~There are 271 death row inmates in Texas.~~
~~There are 263 death row inmates in Texas.~~
~~There are 254 death row inmates in Texas.~~
~~There are 247 death row inmates in Texas.~~
~~There are 227 death row inmates in Texas.~~

There are 232 death row inmates in Texas. Of these, ~~ten~~ six are women. The peak of those sentenced, following the national trend, was in 1999, 460 persons nationally, forty-eight people in Texas.

Birds would no longer startle into flight at my passing.

The phone is ringing when we walk into the house. They made an arrest. Found him in a convenient store buying (what?) four days after. He'd shaved his head somewhere in the in-between. He was still on the bicycle. He gave a full confession. My hands grip the wooden bench during the trial—worn, polished wood curving under my thighs. I want to look at him. I don't want to look at him. I want to see the last person my mother saw, the last person she spoke to. He is closest to her in this way. If I look at him, maybe I could see her. The last of her physical existence still linked to him. But I also don't want to see what she saw.

He brags about it to another inmate. I don't remember if I hear prosecution relay this to the jury or if someone tells me about it afterwards. It comes up in the trial as a matter of culpability. Perhaps he was scared, trying to build a reputation in the first days of incarceration. I was sixteen. He was twenty-six. Life without parole wasn't an option in Texas at the time.

Today I am thirty-seven. He is forty-seven. When I was five, he was fifteen. When I was nine, he was nineteen. I know nothing else. I want to know what he recalls from that day. What are the memories he replays in his mind? I wonder if he is angry or if he's found some sort of peace. I wonder into the space of my mind creating, where time tries to stop, where anything and nothing is possible simultaneously. He's been on death row for twenty years. The average length of time in Texas is twelve years. I know one day the space of wonder will never have a stopping point, only added questions that can never be answered.

(Such frictions may not be chosen. For some, their hearts are grains of sand cloistered in shell-like space. Their secrets grown around them layer upon layer until they are pearls of their own confusions.)

If they ask me I'll deny everything: For so long I've denied the steady, granular accumulation of the dripping, dripping of inner springs. I grow long as stalactites and fragile as time.

Walking back to my room after dinner one of the exit doors between cars is open. The night air rushes past in pure black. It would be easy to lose one's balance—stumble, trip, fall thru an unexpected open door. How long, I wonder, would I tumble before I stopped? My hands instinctually grip the rail wrapped in red and white tape. I close my eyes. The metal floor sends the jolts of the tracks up my legs, my knees and hips, my spine cushions the reverberations. I loosen the grip and begin to feel the vibrations sound through the body, pulse sensation into my ears. Cold wind pricks my cheeks, finds its way through the fibers of my clothes. When I open my eyes again we're slowing into a station. The outskirts of an unfamiliar town, street lamps glow yellow chipped curbs. Old dirty snow piles the road's edges.

My friction is a falling away, an arrival out of numbness. Now when I speak water's break from limestone crusts. My tongue is a long column suspended from the ceiling of some ghostly grotto.

My father tells me one morning while driving to church, a counselor told him to expect a year of grieving for every year they were married. *So I guess I have eighteen more years to go.* He says it like he has no other choice. He has been committed and must serve out the allotted time. The first year gapes the holes left by her. Emptiness highlighted by the details we were afraid of forgetting, but too painful to consistently remember. All time became slotted into before and after, until one day, not long ago, I realize We've lived longer without her than with her. This time before and time after has become balanced by the outstretch of time that lays ahead: a slow incline to the peak, a tumbling fall to the point of ever after, the unknown trek into the after-after.

The Hebrew word for Lord is *adonai*, which has one of its roots in *ehden*, or threshold. Threshold as in: *edge, brink, beginning.* As in: *We begin after we cross the threshold.* Threshold as in: *limit, verge, inception.* As in: *I'm on the verge.* In physiology or psychology, a threshold is the point at which a stimulus is of sufficient intensity to begin to produce an effect. As in: *pain.* Another word for threshold is *limen.* Not to be confused with *liman,* a geological term to describe a muddy marsh near the mouth of a river.

Growing-up our family made biannual pilgrimages to South Padre Island off the coast of Texas. I think one of the major reasons my parents packed three kids, luggage, and coolers into the Grand Marquis on three day weekends was for the sunsets at the dunes. Each night we'd pilgrimage to where the road on the island stopped and hike into the white sand. The island is skinny enough that from the top of the dunes you can look west across the bay towards the mainland and then turn your head east and look across the Gulf towards the Atlantic.

While my parents sat in stillness at the top of a dune and watched the sun draw out departure across open sky like a well-orchestrated concerto, my brothers and I would chase each other in high intensity games of hide-and-go-seek. We became particularly attuned to sliding from the top of a dune like snowboarders without the board.

Right before the sun would set, my father would call us to join them. *Look close and you'll see the green flash,* he'd say. We'd all sit staring at the sun, trying not to blink as it fractured the horizon and slipped beneath the water. *Don't blink. Don't blink or you'll miss it.*

Swells of sand are held whole
by the undulating circuitry
of sea vines. Their green
life force networks from dune to dune
and harbors lizards with crusty brown skin.

Until the sun goes our children
play maneuvers in their vastness,
losing and seeking each other.
They roll with my lost abandon
down slopes silvering in fading light.

My blood pulses a prayer for my abandon
lost sometime ago between tides.
My vision transfixed on a setting sun,
I ceased to be partnered with the landscape
and grew into spectator.

My visits now are brief.

The first years after, we continued to make the trip South. My brothers and I would bring friends, each of us trying to avoid existing in a place with four, where the fifth was so honestly missing. I started walking down the dunes to the Gulf during these years, to touch the water, to touch something greater than me. I remember walking back and looking up towards the dunes, silhouettes lit by the setting sun. I watched my brothers, ages fifteen and seven, and their friends jump to surf down the dune, one by one. Alone at the top of the dune, my father walked away from the edge as far as he could then started running, his arms pumping, his tan stout body moving along the ridge and he leapt, flung his body head first off the side of the dune.

And this is how I remember him. Suspended in air, arms open wide, daring the ground to break his fall, daring the ground to hurt him more than he was hurting. He hit headfirst and tumbled, without control, without trying to stop himself he tumbled as fast as gravity would allow to the ground below.

Since words don't exist
to translate this love anyway
I must speak a language
I never knew I knew before.

Yet I find you make me fluent.
Words lay silent
as my heart whispers
in tongues of love.

Because sensory, motor and cognitive functions are served by multiple pathways the same information is processed simultaneously in different regions of the brain. Because of this, if one path is damaged, other paths may compensate, *at least partially, for the loss.*

Grief is a multifaceted response to loss, particularly when the loss is irrevocable. Although conventionally focused on the emotional response, grief also has physical, cognitive, behavioral, social, and philosophical dimensions. Our brains will often ignite physical responses when faced with psychological issues. We change the paradigms from where we view the world. How we interact with others. Elisabeth Kübler-Ross in her 1969 book, *On Death and Dying,* first discusses the five stages of grief: Denial/Isolation. Anger. Bargaining. Depression. Acceptance. Grief is highly singular in that each individual is wholly responsible for what is happening inside of them and yet it's almost impossible to live in the world, be a part of a family or a community and go through it alone.

Before he killed her she said, *I forgive you and God does too.* I've often wondered when—exactly—did she speak these words. I imagine it was after the initial shock of being attacked. After the hypothalamus sent a message to the adrenal glands to produce adrenaline. After the initial increase in heart rate and respiration. After the muscles in her legs felt heavy and light at the same time. I don't imagine it was her initial response. And I don't imagine she screamed the words. I wonder how close he was. If his ear was near her lips when the words left her mouth. Or was he leaving. Was he walking away, his back turned to her and from the ground, hidden by the tall grass, did she say, *I forgive you. And God does too?*

For a long time I said to myself, *how could I not?* But he never factored into the equation. It wasn't a person that needed forgiving, it was the entire situation. All of the circumstances that led to the consequence at hand. Too many *what ifs* to counter the one big cleft we found ourselves standing on. Life needed forgiving, not him. He became insignificant in the process as soon as punishment was set. What she did do with her words was open the door to acceptance. Acceptance that life, no matter how hard we try or how hard we fight it, will ever be as it was. Forgiveness comes after. After the necessary stops, cycling through, denial into anger into depression, they catch us thick and flatten into our road ahead. Returning, each time a new experience, each time familiar from before, remembering. Sometimes they catch us whole and their richness provides movement. Sometimes they catch us stuck. Without feeling. Just a body in motion. Time dictates we are always moving forward, even when grief dictates we stop.

When you go I hold a gray dove in my hands and feel in his feathered softness the memory of flight.

Getting dressed for her funeral at sixteen

The black lamé fabric rips at the seam when I pull the zipper up
    the length of my torso

Barefoot, stockingless : I stand alone in front of the mirror
    Mother, this is the only black dress I own

The night before my senior year in high school, a couple of days after the funeral, my mother's mother called me from Baton Rouge. She said, *Tomorrow you are going to wake-up and go to school and I will go to work because that's what we have to do.* I don't remember much from the months that followed. I do remember family friends sleeping on the couch. The casseroles stacked high in our freezer. Every evening after school, after cross-country practice, I'd remove one of the perfectly portioned meals for four and preheat the oven to 425. Repeat the following night. Motions void of dipping below functionality. Hug father when he can't stop crying. Listen when six-year old brother questions if there is a God. Run more, try to stay awake in class, run harder, have asthma attacks, run. Graduate. Drink too much. Smoke too much. Wear her watch. Graduate college. Wear her jewelry. Through the motions. Become the parent of my brothers, because my father can't. Become the parent of my father. Do not stare at mothers having coffee with their daughters. Travel. Do the things she would have done. Do the things she never would have. I can't call her when I'm pregnant. Or when I miscarry. I dip my hands into the bloody water of the toilet bowl and scoop out the barely formed fetus. Wrap it in toilet paper and bury it in the garden next to the laughing concrete buddha.

I wing my way on the echoes of songs held sweet

If we were to unravel the DNA of our body and cast the thread into the night sky, it would travel past the moon and the red dirt of Mars, past the storms of Jupiter, and the ice rings of Saturn, the many moons of Uranus, the winds of Neptune, past Pluto before circling back around and traveling back to Earth where we would be standing, holding the end of the thread in one hand and reaching towards the sky with the other to catch our existence, a lasso of time and stardust. The knowledge of the past held within the quaking threads of living—our eternal exclamation.

in the night and blend with the clouds that hug a far horizon.

The morning is at stasis—a thin air's breath
drawn out long and delicate as a spider's spinning.

The dry creek bed feeds like an artery through outcroppings of pine.
I have journeyed such distance to sit on this seat of grace.

But the land belies the passion that comes in the course of torrent flooding—
the upheaved roots, the jumble of rock, a weathered feel of smooth bark.

We are blood-cousins this red-dirt bank and I,
resigned in a wisdom that comes on this clear blue morning.

In order for the transcontinental railroad to connect from Sacramento to the existing rails of the East, almost two thousand miles of track had to be laid through the mountain ranges of the Sierras and the Rockies. In total, nineteen tunnels were carved out of the granite mountains. Tunnel No. 6, through Donner Pass in Eastern California, taps in as the longest at 1,750 feet. In the winter of 1866-67 it's estimated that 8,000 men, worked in three round-the-clock shifts to create the tunnel. Teams worked inward from both sides and two more teams tunneled into the middle of the would-be-tunnel from the top then worked outward. They hand chiseled holes into the granite, packed the holes with gun powder, and exploded small sections at a time. Two feet of progression a day was considered good progress. Eventually, nitro-glycerine was experimented with and increased the progression to about 3.82 feet per day. The blacksmith who set-up shop near the tunnel had a steady stream of hammers and chisels to re-forge. Men returning to camp for rest and food and a re-vamping of their tools. The transcontinental rail took six years to complete and on May 10, 1869 the East and the West met at Promontory, Utah with a golden spike, cars filled with reporters, politicians, and cases of champagne. In June 1876, the Transcontinental Express set the record of eighty-three hours and thirty-nine minutes to make the trip between New York City and San Fransisco.

It is the consistency of things slipping into pallor that brings me to this field.

Thunder is the sound of pressure around the lightning bolt. The air rapidly expanding. Lightning always creates two channels: from the clouds to the ground—from the ground to the clouds. The second path creates so much electricity in such a short amount of time the air has no time to expand. Compressed. Particles explode outward, a shock wave in every direction, an explosion. Aloud, re-sounding rupture.

The hardest part was knowing he went back. The biggest *what if* came from her movement. He was leaving. The report reads he heard her moving and saw a witness ap-proaching. So he returns. To her beaten, bloody body. *Moth-er, don't move. Be still.*

In the photograph she is smiling, her chin turned towards the light, her forty-seven year old hair died dirty blonde, blue-green eyes my youngest brother inherited. Her smile is not closed, it shows teeth, spreads her lips wide, raises her cheekbones. The photograph was taken in our back-yard when film still needed to be processed. After an after-noon summer storm, the butterfly weed and roses glisten in the background along a wooden fence. The concrete birdbath sits just out of view, rain water collected to fill the belly of a sparrow. The photo hung in the hallway between bedrooms, next to school photos with books and fake ap-ples and the rodeo photo of us years younger. My brothers and I sit with our mother on a bucking stuffed bull, my father hangs from the horns, we are all open mouthed, frozen in joyful chaos, staring into the camera.

Here the moths will radar my presence and catch the dust of decay on their heavy wings.

I don't know who took the photo off of the wall and out of the frame to make a copy for the newspaper. To accompany the final words summarizing her life. I wonder if they cleaned the glass in the process. Wiped the collected dust before once again hanging the frame back on the wall. It's the first image I see when I think of her, a headshot saved photo to my memory. I've recalled the photo so often I don't actually know if it had just rained or if it was dew on a Houston morning, if it was summer or spring, or if the roses had just bloomed. I don't know which details are real and which ones I've created to fill the blank spaces. And is it better to fill blank spaces with details in order to find a sense of wholeness or are holes of uncertainty, blips of blank, a more complete reality?

The contract between citizens is if you break the code of humanity and commit the crime of murder, you secede your right of freedom. Depending on where you live, death will end your life sooner rather than later. Michael Selsor served thirty- six years on death row, the longest amount of time to be served between conviction and execution. Nationally, the average amount of time between sentencing and execution has increased from six years, in 1984, to sixteen years, in 2012. Many who oppose the Death Penalty advocate for Life Without Parole. Selsor is quoted as saying, *the only difference between death and life without parole is one you kill me now, the other one you kill me later. There's not even a shred of hope. There's no need to even try to muster up a seed of hope because you're just gonna die of old age in here...* Death Row Phenomenon refers to the harmful effects on inmates. It includes such conditions as extended exposure in solitary confinement and the mental anxiety of an impending death. Death Row Syndrome on the other hand refers to the psychological illness that results from Death Row Phenomenon. This is of course a matter of perspective. Everyone has an impending death—with walls or without. Some of us are simply more aware of this one certainty—with walls or without.

My everything has left me.

The arguing points on both sides seem to stem from fear. The kind of fear that comes from the same place hope hides. In the case of Life Without Parole the fear that one day the convicted might earn parole or a governor might reduce the sentence. Or hope they are afforded days to perhaps, find redemption. And in the case of Death, the fear they might be exonerated or experience anything but punishment before they die. Hope, perhaps, they will die before finding peace or hope they have found peace before they die.

In his famous treaty *Of Crimes and Punishment*, Cesare Beccaria writes, *Let us consult the human heart, and there we shall find the foundation of the sovereign's right to punish; for no advantage in moral policy can be lasting which is not founded on the indelible sentiments of the heart of man. Whatever law deviates from this principle will always meet with a resistance which will destroy it in the end; for the smallest force continually applied will overcome the most violent motion communicated to bodies.* Malcolm Gladwell makes the argument that many social issues might be deduced down to weak-link or strong-link problems. For example the Industrial Revolution was a weak-link phenomena due to the fact that Britain had more backyard tinkerers than other areas of the world at the time. There wasn't one superstar who brought the revolution into play, but rather the aptitude of the entire area was elevated thus leading to the proletarian discovery of James Watt. Likewise, Gladwell argues, the education system is a weak-link

I stand boneless while the moths circle in mute procession

problem. We are only as strong as the faultiest of our educational directives. Education is the periodic table of society—solid standing across all elements ensures stability. A society doesn't grow in suppression, or opposition. A society grows as one unit. Even if denied by the whole, or by all, society like self is inherently connected. In a sermon given on Christmas Eve in 1967, Dr. Martin Luther King testifies to the belief: *We are all caught in an inescapable network of mutuality, tied into a single garment of destiny. Whatever affects one directly, affects all indirectly. We are made to live together because of the interrelated structure of reality.* One body, our body, moving together.

The verb *to serve* stems from the Latin word *servire*, to be a slave or the noun *servus,* slave. The definition today has broadened in its action to include: *to be of use, to be worthy of trust, to prove adequate*, and *to work through.* Serving time, it seems, is the base remedy for a shattered psyche.

We both have been serving time. My prison made of hours and days, graduations and finish lines, weddings and births, holidays. Each joyous moment simultaneously a prison. I was a freshman in college when I realized my mother would never witness any of the marked events of my life. It struck me quite suddenly while filing papers in the financial aid office where I worked. It seemed her loss would give forever; a life sentence.

past the horizon where the sun has gone, the consistency of it.

Hollowed out of heaven stars point their light toward my eyes.

Sometimes it all stops. On the tracks, pitch
black every direction, just the memory of starlight. A freight train needs to pass. We wait. For
what seems like years. The tracks our only indicator we once were—Sometimes the darkness
is sudden, a tunnel. Into a mountain. Granite
exploded, chiseled, seasoned by time and train
exhaust and water that seeps from inside the
earth, from somewhere deeper still, I press my
forehead to the glass my eyes reflected back to
me, cheekbones inherited. I see nothing when
we're in the middle. It's only when approaching
the other side, where light's reach brims, can the
frozen columns of ice dripping from the ceiling
be seen. Temporary stalagmites formed out of
situation.

I am amazed each time I see

stars journeying their brilliance across December skies.

Early in the work of memory Freud postulated that there are different neurons for different purposes. In the case of perception, the way we perceive the physical world around us, the synaptic connections of the neuron are fixed. And in neurons concerned with memory, the connections change in their strength depending on the amount of time given to that particular circuit. It seems reasonable to think that if we recall a memory often enough it will become a fixed perception, a cairn for our thoughts. Awareness is a synonym for perception: an ability to understand the worth, quality, or importance of something. When we have perception, we have awareness.

The more we perceive from the world around us, the larger and more intricate the map for these perceptions becomes inside our brains. It is possible to learn so much detail about the world around us that the hippocampus, where memory is saved, becomes larger. When we travel certain roads often and get to know the intricacies—where the sidewalk cracks, the dent of a mailbox, a scar on the body of a loved one—they become landmarks. These places we know become the shelf from which we draw details when our brain doesn't have time to fully perceive. Light on the retina, the vibration of the fibers in the ear drum, the sinus cavities of the nose, are all but a piece that contribute to the brain's map. When something doesn't make sense, when there is a rift in our perception, we will draw from what we know and try to give it sense. It's how we find our reality—the getting there.

In physics, movement is described as any change in the position of an object with respect to time as a reference point. Time is just space between one moment and another. Between ourselves then and ourselves now. Between me and you. Time is the movement we cannot control. We are simply along for the ride, existing only in this moment. Sometimes standing still. Sometimes leaping. Sometimes falling. But always here. Right here, from one cleft to another.

I am homesick for a place that no longer exists. A place that stopped existing years ago, reachable only in my mind. But this place that no longer exists, the home lost, has less to do with losing another and more with the idea that no matter what has happened in life, if we have lost or not, we can never return to before. It's all memory. In his play, *The Milk Train Doesn't Stop Here Anymore,* Tennessee Williams writes, *Has it ever occurred to you that it's all memory, except for the present moment you can hardly catch it going.* Life is all memory, contained within the cells of our brains. Family is simply sharing the same memories or as Zach Braff writes in his first screenplay, *Garden State*: *Family is missing the same imaginary place.* Missing the same moments which ultimately is missing the same emotions. The same imaginary place inside.

The word *volve* comes from the latin word *volvere* meaning to roll or turn over, especially in the mind. It's where *evolve and revolve* stem from. In the case of *evolve* the "e" stems from Latin to mean *out* or *away*. As in, *eclipse, eliminate, eternal*. The *re* of *revolve* also stems from Latin meaning *again* or *backwards*. As in, *record, remain, refuse*. Respond. Our brains are constantly changing and connecting. Regions of the prefrontal cortex are updated every five to eight seconds. This means from the first breath we take to the last we expel, our brain is changing itself. Recalculating. Forming new memories, filling in the pieces that are missing. Building new pathways, or reinforcing old ones. Existence as revolution. Evolution, a reduction into existence.

Texas was the last state to sign into legislation the option of life without parole for those facing the Death Penalty. The law is not retroactive. A violent motion communicated to bodies.

The Jewish prayer verse said at the time of death is called the *Shema* which translates as LISTEN. The *Shema* is also spoken upon waking in the morning and falling asleep at night—creating a line of intention. An intent to listen. Among pine and concrete angels, listen. The definition of *hear* takes up a page and a half in the second edition of the Oxford English Dictionary. Entry number twelve of the definition reads, *to have heard of or to be aware.* We cannot be aware if we do not hear. We cannot hear if we do not listen.

Theodosius Dobzhansky, one of the founders of the modern synthesis of evolutionary theory, writes, *Nothing in biology makes sense except in light of evolution…without that light it becomes a pile of sundry facts some of them interesting or curious but making no meaningful picture as a whole.* If we were to stretch out the veins and arteries and capillaries in our body, the pathways that carry our blood would cover over 60,000 miles. The earth's circumference at the equator is 24,901 miles which means we could each circle our blood 2.4 times around the thickest part of earth. Our nervous system is over forty-five miles long. The pathways created from one neuron to another, the length of feeling in your big toe to your brain, the pit in your stomach to the breath in your lungs. The distance between the bayou where she was found and the Polunsky Unit where he sits is ninety miles. Two bodies worth of nerves.

Glistening as a lock of silver hair fallen askew the water braids
and weaves to the creek at our feet below.

Hard as we stare into the upward growth of stone and moss
we cannot tell from where the birth of this bright stream.

Outside the frozen stream passes by under the window—blown glass, a green hewn murk frosted still, the grass—burnt sienna, emerges from the bank leaning slightly in one direction. As if a frigid wind has gusted everything into silence. It's hard to imagine this land at a different time when the days are long and the water, warm, sways the tall grass from underneath. The sun low in the sky, begins its descent. It seems the days end, just when they're beginning. From where the sun is now a shimmer casts over the frozen water—a luster of reflection. The stream becomes a river, still, frozen, occasionally a break in the surface where the ice has started to melt, where the water is deepest, and I can see ripples of movement ebbing and flowing underneath.

The source is held in secrecy. Of some things we see is enough to know. Water slips in sheets

across memories of rocks and leaves eternal smoothness. Hypnotic chords of foaming, falling, freeing hold us in perfect harmony far into the night.

Sufism is a branch of Islam that follows the teachings of the Qur'an. The religion of the Sufi, like the root of most religions, is Love. The path to reach Truth, Understanding, God—stems out of this Love. Love is the path; loss is often the way. Rumi, one of Sufism's major teachers writes, *Sorrow…violently sweeps everything out of your house, so that new joy can find space to enter. It shakes the yellow leaves from the bough of your heart, so that fresh, green leaves can grow in their place. It pulls up the rotten roots, so that new roots hidden beneath have room to grow.* But joy doesn't immediately follow sorrow. The in-between is what matters. The in-between is the process, that which creates who we are. Being in the in-between, allowing emptiness to be the space inhabited, to become the new way, holds space for when the joy arrives.

In writing about why America latched on to trains early in the 20th century Don Ball, Jr. observes that humans *instinctually find that most things which move are inherently more interesting than most things which are fixed.* We are meant to move. Our bodies, our minds, our emotions. It's against our nature to be fixed, to be stuck. Sometimes necessary, but against the instincts that make us human. The cells of our bodies regenerate at different rates. Skin renews at a different rate than the fibers of our muscles. The oldest part of our physical existence is the cortical neuron held within the cortex of the brain. Abstract concepts like Justice and voluntary movements like dancing live here. This is also where the pathways to all of the senses converge. The hippocampus, held within the cortex, generates about 1,400 new neurons a day. Our brain constantly is supplied with the opportunity to create, to connect memories to

When we first started, Megaera seemed so far. But we came out of the desert

the senses. When we store memories long-term it's the hippocampus that files the memories away to the appropriate area of the brain for later retrieval.

One of the expressions of the Sufi is the practice of revolving—like confessing in Catholicism or sitting shiva in Judaism—the Sufi spins. Often accompanied by music, the breath of a reed flute and the beat of a floor drum, is the ritual of *Sema*. The *Sema* is not a singular event of one person spinning, but communal, each person spinning individually together. In flowing white garments representing the ego's shroud, soft slippers on the feet and a hat made of camel hair representing the ego's tombstone, the Sufi tilts their head twenty-three and a half degrees, just as the earth is tilted in space, and begins to spin their body. Beginning with the arms folded in across the chest, across the heart, they begin to spin, as the earth spins, and together they spin in a circle as the moon revolves around the earth, as the earth revolves around the sun, the arms open, the right reaching towards the heavens, the left reaching towards the earth, they spin, as the electrons, neutrons, and protons spin inside the atoms of the body, as the blood circulates, the Sufi honors the inevitable revolution. A dance of sweeping, a dance of memory, a dance of how.

I Google *How to contact someone on death row.* There are several organizations committed to connecting Death Row inmates with pen pals. The first result is from brethren.org, an organization who claims they are *continuing the work of Jesus. Peacefully. Simply. Together.* The second, Human Writes, is an organization based out of the UK, *a non-profit humanitarian organization which befriends people on death row in the USA.* He's not listed on any of the websites requesting contact. In fact only thirty-eight of the male prisoners on Death Row in Texas are. There are introductions from those listed. I read through a few. Several proclaim they are the victims of bad attorneys. Mostly though, they are looking for people to connect with. He's not listed. I want him to be. I don't want him to be. I realize I'm looking for effects. I'm trying to find threads of meaning from the crossroad where we met.

I read in *The Internet Journal of Criminology* that death row inmates *recreate individually, often spend twenty-three hours alone and have individual sixty square feet cells.* That's about half the size of a parking space. *Everything, apart from a metal sanitation unit, is grey concrete; including the bed, stool and walls. There is one slim window but this provides so little natural light that the cell is illuminated by strip lighting. Although the prisoner spoke about conditions being sometimes eerily silent, he also described how it could also be unbearably noisy; the sound of keys rattling, toilets flushing, pipes gargling and prisoner's voices echoing through the labyrinth of cells. Other prisoners complained that the sudden clashes and bangs that penetrated their walls caused them to feel constantly unnerved; their unease owing partly to the fact that they did not know where the noises were originating from.* There is a list of upcoming executions in Texas. Eight names in the next five months. He's not listed.

and that time-splintered August when we sanctified ourselves outside of Normandy.

I have questions I want to ask him. My husband says don't underestimate the magnitude of what's lurking underneath. But, there are things I want to know. I wonder if he has found a place of peace or a place of despair, a sense of hope or existence in denial. I want him to have suffered; but I also want him to have found grace. Somehow, if he has then two lives were not frozen. Ultimately, it doesn't change anything. I know the meaningless of the act remains without reason and applying reason simply changes the lens from where I'm viewing. But I want him to have found meaning. It somehow gives purpose to the prisons we've been living in. I speak to a woman who has experience connecting prisoners to the family members of their victims. She asks me what I want to say to him. She asks if I need to express forgiveness. I don't. She says, *What hasn't been realized is the reality of the other human being.* And this is true; and echoes into the space of my heart. He is but a small piece fractured. A kaleidoscope form that has recently come to focus. The intent of my moving forward did not include him. Not until now. Another friend tells me, *forgiveness is a selfish act.* It's not about the one doing the forgiving, it's always about the one being forgiven.

There are three pieces to the language instinct: to speak, to understand, and to repeat. As children we repeat words spoken to us, we listen, we imitate in sound and intonation. We speak and eventually begin to understand. The

You have always been worthy of a poem.

lack of this language instinct is called aphasia. Wernicke's aphasia is a disorder of the brain causing the affected individual an inability to comprehend language—both words heard and words spoken. While the intonation and rhythm of the sentences are correct, the words are random and mixed with made-up words. Mlab runs tomorrow, thunder pane, mortoo because. In Broca's aphasia however, the affected person is able to process the words, but unable to produce responding communication.

In the letter, I ask him to respond. It would have been enough to have just sent the letter, but I needed to know he'd heard my words.

It is a devotion I pay you through time.

You cannot use logic to get out of a situation where there was none used in the first place. There is not logic in senseless death. Kevin Young writes, *To lose someone close to you is to enter an experience no amount of forethought or hindsight can free you from. You must live through grief. You cannot outsmart it, nor think through the fact of someone's being gone, and forever. You must survive the sorrow.* You must survive the sorrow. The illogical sense filled death. Improbable to escape. Even in my denial filled delusions, I know there is no getting out of death. It is complete in its rift. For those of us left, there is only the climbing deeper inside, beyond logic, into the sorrow swept self. The movement of grief rocking us into stillness, stilling us into hope that we might emerge once more.

After the second punishment trial he asked to address the family. The *Houston Chronicle* reported, after the jury was excused he *tearfully apologized to Adleman's family. "I'm sorry," [he] said, sobbing, "...for causing y'all so much pain that day. ...I think about what she said to me, that she forgave me and did I know God. I couldn't understand why she did that but I didn't know God then. I looked for answers but I can tell you now I know God now, and I know I took a special person away from you, and I'm sorry for that." A family member replied...* I can only imagine this was my father. My brothers and I did not attend the second trial, nor would we have been the impromptu spokesperson. I imagine my father stood from the wooden bench where he had been sitting during the trial and looked at the man in front of him. I imagine my father's lips twitched before he spoke, as they do, piercing into thought before he says something poignant or heartfelt. The paper reports the family member said, *We thank you for your apology. Thank you.* But this is not what actually happened. I was informed by a family friend that the family member who spoke was my grandmother, my mother's mother, not my father. The friend said the courtroom was almost empty, my father had just left, and she was waiting with my grandparents to drive them back to the hotel where they were staying during the trial. She said after he spoke the words there was a large silence. A waiting. An uncomfortable waiting. My grandmother stood and *spoke politely and bitterly. She thanked him, as any strong and civil southern grand dame would do, but she did not mean acceptance and certainly not forgiveness. That was clear.* I prefer the memory of my father I created. This memory, though invented, contains a level of decorum that gives permission to wholeness. It opens the door in kindness to whatever might be lurking behind. The words a genuine retrieval, a reflection of her, illuminated in the emptiness. Strength embodied. But the reality is the response was terse, but not clean, laden in grime protecting the still raw hurt, the pain too fresh to remove. It is only because of the distance of time that I can allow myself to believe in the created memory.

He will spend the next twelve years appealing the sentence of Capital Punishment until the U.S. Supreme Court denies his appeal. This was in 2014. A sentence is defined by a group of words that expresses, questions, commands, or wishes a statement. They begin with a capital letter and end with a period, a question mark, or an exclamation point. Sentence is also the punishment given by law. It too can end with a period, a question mark, or an exclamation point.

Then I knew you would be a poem because you too have a pilgrim's heart.

Concentration camp survivor and philosopher, Viktor Frankl asked himself while in the concentration camp, *Has all this suffering, this dying around us, a meaning? For, if not, then ultimately there is no meaning to survival; for a life whose meaning depends upon such a happenstance—as whether one escapes or not—ultimately would not be worth living at all.* The Neuron Doctrine, inferred by Santiago Ramón y Cajal, states the electrical web formed between the axon terminals of neurons are not random. Discriminately neurons form connections with certain nerve cells and not others. There is a constant choice. After a while these choices become habits recognized as patterns that create the framework of who we are. The more the framework is utilized and the pathways are ignited, the stronger they become. Without connections between cells there is no memory. There is no us.

After the death of his son, Ralph Waldo Emerson refers to the grief as courting suffering. He writes, *there are moods in which we court suffering, in the hope that here, at least, we shall find reality, sharp peaks and edges of truth.* By feeling we find truth. By feeling we know in this moment we exist. To be alive and not feel is contradictory to the very essence of living. The preposition of *a,* as in *alive,* is a reduced form of the Old English preposition *on,* meaning *in, into,* or *toward.* In life. Into life. Toward life. To be alive doesn't require constantly being on, but rather moving towards an existence. It's messy. Feeling truth—feeling emotions we don't want to feel. That's vulnerability. Feeling unsafe inside ourselves, moving into what we don't know, places we haven't been. Guided only by the simple desire to be clean.

We step across the depths now.

The acceptance of responsibility for one's own life is as Joan Didion writes, *the source from which self-respect springs.* My mother taped sheets of paper that read *Choose Joy* all over the house—on bathroom mirrors, closet doors, inside kitchen cabinets—we grew up with a constant reminder to choose. Nobody took the sheets of paper down after she was gone. A constant reminder to move towards Joy.

I wonder if he has any whys. I wonder if he has whys to bear the hows. Nietzsche writes, *if we have our own why in life, we shall get along with almost any how.* This is what I want to know. It seems to follow logic that freedom is easier to grasp and experience if you have full use of your life. But I think it's the opposite. We realize what we miss once it's gone, or once we experience the opposite. *I never saw the morning till I stayed up all night,* Tom Waits croons. Viktor Frankyl proposes, *freedom is only part of the story and half of the truth. Freedom is but the negative aspect of the whole phenomenon whose positive aspect is responsibleness.* The laws that govern are meant to provide equilibrium in society. We are responsible for following the laws, but more importantly, we are responsible for our perceptions—our personal laws that govern our individual equilibriums. And when basic choices like sleeping, food, fresh air are removed— what happens to perception? Is it not our responsibility to find the why within the how?

I've had the dream before. She returns, alive and into the house we all used to share. She's been on an adventure,

The world has become a trinket and we lose it whenever our hands touch.

visiting far-off lands, living with other families. She returns and it's always disorienting. I have a need to take care of her. At first, it was like welcoming your favorite, eccentric Aunt to Thanksgiving dinner. She was carefree, her hair grown long, wanderer's eyes. And my father is sadness, burdened by this earthbound life. They aren't together. She doesn't move back in. Even in my dreams we don't return to before. She no longer wholly belongs here. I used to wish I could dream her. I would think about her before bed in hopes my brain would return to her—anything. Her voice, her smile, her touch. She recently visited and I woke angry. Unreasonably at her control to appear and disappear when she chooses. A pigmented representation of reality.

The pigment of grief is often so blue it's black, like a storm sky reflected in the the deep ocean. Like the muddy bottom of a bayou. Pigments are defined in their essence by choosing which colors of the light spectrum will be absorbed, thus changing the reflection. The earliest known pigments are dated to 2.6 million years ago. Red ochre and carbon black both are linked to this time. Pigments are classified by their permanence and their stability. When a pigment is not permanent it is called fugitive. Fugitive colors fade over time or when exposed to light, they become void of any color. Pigments can only subtract wavelengths from the source light. They can never add new ones.

Poetry is here with us escaping in the dark beyond Neptune.

I will catch it—I will weave it like a basket, an art long-remembered from my mother in Egypt.

My mother was working on a new play about Miriam in the last months of her life. Miriam, sister of Moses, who hid her brother in the tall grass by the river in order to save him from the Pharaoh's order to kill all newborn boys. Miriam, who danced and sang and played her timbrel after they crossed the Red Sea. Miriam, who died in the desert, without water. Her name means *bitter*, but bitter as in *strong*—like grief makes us strong. The name stems from the verb *to change*, as bitterness is a cause to the effect of change. Miriam—roots out of the noun *sea* or *hot springs*, as in *bitter waters or waters of strength*. My mother told my father she'd run by herself that evening to mull over some lines in her head.

There is a concept in yoga and meditation called *tapas*. It translates into English as *the fire from within*. As the *light* or *luster* inside. Luster, a soft glow—especially off of a reflective surface. It's where our intuition stems from, it's where awareness lives. The fire inside that can burn uncontrollably in rage decimating everything into ash. Or the fire that can be controlled by the mind, by breath, by consciously allowing whatever is holding us back to burn. To create space inside for other emotions, other experiences. To burn into the luster of reflection. To create a beauty of emptiness.

The four of us started dancing after, not in the very first of after when silence filled our mouths and hearts, but later when we couldn't hear each other over the noise of our thoughts. When there was too much to say and nothing left to say. We blasted *The World at Large* and moved. In my empty living room, in my father's backyard, in my brother's jeep we rose our timbrels and beat in defiance. Each of us so different in our beings, forged out of the circumstance of bayou waste—we are tumbled stones caught: in the night sky. Geoff likes to spin his body and occupy the entire surrounding space. I too fall in this category and when we dance together a six hundred square foot area is sometimes not enough. Zach sways through the shoulders, drops his head, keeps his arms in close. Often his eyes are closed, his feet glued to the ground. Our father dances with his whole body, though it's more of an arm pumping, knee bending bop. The four of us refuse to let go of the other. And perhaps that is what family means—holding on even when it hurts, unable to let go because even if you did the others are holding on to you. Holding on to you and you're holding on to them and everyone is falling together into the space of tomorrow.

I am a dark weaver. Beyond Pluto silence becomes sound

Below the small window and the plate that says *Watch Your Step,* there is a rectangle pad where a handle might be. It reads *Press to Open* and the metal door slides to one side. I step into the space between cars : the joints of movement that absorb the jolts and bumps of the track. The door slides shut behind me. I can feel the outside air seeping in from between the metal plates, the smell of diesel exhaust. I stand between the two cars, teetering between thresholds. Between where I came from and where I'm headed. Frozen. If the train were to disconnect, would it be here? This space between space, this cocoon of metal latches and plates holding one car to the next.

and this poem will rustle like reeds in the Nile when I hand it to you.

The difference between comets and asteroids is over water. Both were formed early in our history when metals and space dust and rock were swirling around the sun. Comets formed further away from the sun and contain ice which remains frozen in the depths of space. As a comet approaches the sun, flying overhead for us to witness, the ice melts and vaporizes into a tail, a singular blaze traversing the heavens. Asteroids, on the other hand, formed near the sun, all of the steam compressed of being. During an asteroid's lifetime it might collide with other asteroids and be sent into similar orbits around the sun. These groups are known as families. The OED first defines family as *the servants of a house or a household.* We serve the place where we live through communion of space. The second definition broadens the scope by harnessing the definition to a physicality—*those who live under the same roof.* We are family because we share the same space. And the third definition removes the physical requirement of living together and broadens even further to *parents and their children, across time and space, as well as those bound together by blood or affinity.* We are connected because we share the same path; we share the same blood.

Do you need to express forgiveness? I don't. But I don't know that I do. Or that I ever will. But this has nothing to do with the other. My decision to move forward is no less dependent on him than I am on his. Occasionally, I still feel the remnants of anger, in the pit of my stomach, a nauseating wave—in the ache of my heart, a dull pain. Like lightning, gone before I fully turn my focus, but evident by the charred grass. More than anger and a raw heart, there is loneliness. A loneliness of space that cannot and will not ever be filled. A loneliness for a time that will never be again. But then, all time is a dance between before and after spinning on the footing of now. Time lends itself to healing—it is often the principal weaving itself through a listening heart and the space of mind. Bodies become prayers offered in gratitude.

Archytas of Tarentum, born in 428 B.C., was the first to suggest the universe has no boundary, perhaps the first to suggest infinity. He imagined someone walking to the edge of the universe and throwing a spear. The spear, he argued, would have to land somewhere, and that somewhere, was still within the universe. That someone could walk again to the spear and throw once more into the void and again the spear would land within the boundaries of our universe. An eternity of expansion. But what of the beginning? According to the Vedas, the most ancient texts of our human history, before there were the stars or the planets or the sun, before there was creation or destruction or the space between, there was Aditi. In sanskrit, Aditi, translates as *boundless*. Song does not not sing to Aditi, but rather song exists because of her. Aditi is the song. Representation of harmony and rhythm, of lyrics and silence. The root of her name stems from *da, to bind.* The *A* is, *un,* as in *unbind.* To not be bound—to be free—to be freedom. In visual representations, Aditi carries a trishul, a three pointed sword, like that of an ornate pitchfork. The trines have different meanings: past, present, future or physical being, sensual being, mental being. The trishul a representation of us each—the person of who we've been along the continuous timeline—existing then, existing now, existence as future self. Scientists think information might be what's expanding the universe. The more our cells collide, our thoughts interact, the ways of being intercede—the further we stretch the possibility of existence. Bits of thought as stars, light traveling, stringing into perception. The nebulas of mind, the supernovas of thought, the dark matter inside shining to light. If information is energy and memories are currency—where do you source your future? If my world collides into yours and we create a new fantasia, will our breath support remembrance?

We have collided. Of all the universes available, we have found one another in this one. Of all the lifetimes to share, we are living together in this one. And for a short time we share this path, orbiting truth, hurling through the expanse of mind and memory. Trying to be better than when we first started, or at least return to the freedom of our base. I survive. You survive too. Because we are the same. You and I. Of the same matter. Our presence allows for connection across time and space, untethered by physical form. Memory, the hum of the universe. Silent until we listen. And even when we hear, it is not with our ears but with the vibrations of our cells. Death will always be an eternal vibration, between the OMs of monks and hum of starlight. Life is temporal, vibrating between Neptune's orbit and a cave's echo.

Maggie Nelson says we will always revisit the same subjects in our writing. In our processing. Perhaps the loss of my mother followed by the loss of my father will aways be the place I revisit. They are, after all, my story. But like a memory recalled time and time again, loss transforms into new tracks of exploration. Tracks where my mother's voice is heard and released, where my father returns to life, where the shell of perception is escaped. If all possibilities once were, then the possibility of what might be lays infinitely ahead.

I thought I wanted answers. I thought knowledge of facts, information like how he spends his time behind bars and where he came from might bring sense, might illuminate meaning to the whole meaningless act. But facts bring no more logic into an emotionally charged existence than speculation does with love. When I left the PO Box and walked past the woman admiring the wine-colored gloves and the teenagers on the corner, I started the process of telling my father and two brothers I'd written the letter. That he wrote back. What was a wholly singular act for my path suddenly involved all of us when communication was made. My journey is their journey, even if ancillary—we choose to remain atoms revolving around the other. We've never talked about him, about his personhood. About the very real facts and emotions of his existence or the very real facts and emotions of our individual existences with grief. Early on we filled the space with alcohol and tears— pickled the anger and sadness into the isolated dark, dank cellars of us. When I tell my father he listens. He tells me of his own journey of checking the Texas Death Row Execution schedule over the years. Of his wondering and without hesitation he speaks the words that will alter our relationship. He becomes the parent once more, holds the hand I didn't know needed holding, and says, "I'd like to read the letter. If it's OK with you. If you want to share it with me. I'd like to see what he has to say, if he's changed. I hope he has. You know, you hope everyone changes for the better." I want to catch the next plane and fly home to where he is. Viktor Frankyl writes, *We must not forget that we may also find meaning in life even when confronted with a hopeless situation, when facing a fate that cannot be changed.*

Meaning, he proposes, comes out of experiencing. Experiencing something like Truth. Beauty. Nature. *Or, last but not least, by experiencing another human being in his very uniqueness— by loving him.* By sharing the human experience in all of its ugliness. Loving through the layers to the core of another.

The snow that started falling on that walk home didn't stop falling till May; and the ground between my brother and me didn't begin to thaw until October. Even now, there are words unspoken, not yet breached. Words that still linger in our throats, words that have survived the years by not being brought into the light, feeding on the darkness, perpetuated inside by our own thoughts and emotions. Words that might never form into spoken reality. And that's ok. As long as the unspoken words don't interfere with the realness of what is—the now of love. The letter is still unopened, filed away in a folder labeled *life.* I'm not sure when or if I'll ever be ready to open the envelope and I'm acutely aware of the imbalance of this decision. But for the moment, I know the words I needed to speak were heard. The synapse fired complete.

I've been walking the cars for years now. Back and forth, from one car into the next and then back again. The train always moving. Always moving forward even when I was moving in the opposite direction. Even when I stopped. I head to the very back of the train. I walk through the dining car, the booths are empty, baskets of butter on each table. The cars are filled with people, each seat taken by a recent addition. But as I continue to walk back, through the cars, the people become less. They spread themselves out across entire rows. I see a man who reminds me of my father. He's wearing a Led Zeppelin baseball hat and nods as I walk by. The woman I've seen since I boarded the train, her three young children always on her heels, steps out of the aisle so I may pass. Each door slides open when I press the button and cross into that space between. One swoosh into the next, from threshold to threshold, from car to car. The noise from outside seems to lessen as I move back, the wind outside, the general hum of the engine becomes further away. One car is completely empty except for a young girl staring out the window, hair in her face escaped from the ponytail. Approaching the last car, I press the button to enter. There are no seats, just the same blue carpet and windows as the others. A pile of lilies are stacked on the floor. I walk to the back of the car, the very back of the train, and press my face against the glass. The tracks roll out from underneath us, one wooden tie after another, two silver lines precisely measured carrying the weight across. And next to the door, propped up in the corner, as if this is where it belongs, as if there were no other space for it to exist except for here, the concrete birdbath. In the back of my mind, as the cornerstone for all that I know.

EPILOGUE

Homes in ancient Greece and Rome held, at their center, a fire that burned continuously. At night, the fire was contained within the burning coals by covering with ash and in the morning fresh twigs were added to build the flame. When the fire of a home went out, it was synonymous with the death of a family. The constant fire was an homage and a prayer to ancestors. To those spirits who walked the earth before. During a month spent on Lake Bacalar near the border of Mexico and Belize, while studying meditation and yoga and philosophy, I took part in a traditional Indian sweat lodge.

Climbing inside the teepee, our temporary womb, we prayed for each of the directions: East, South, West, North, the Sky, the Earth, and the Creator. We prayed for the trauma and pains of our family seven generations before and seven generations after: a recapitulation of karma. The fire burned in the center of the teepee and we sat in a circle singing, chanting, offering, confessing, internalizing, clearing, purging, sweating, until all seven directions had been honored and explored and then we crawled, as the first species may have crawled out of the lagoon, and collapsed on the shore of the lake, beneath the stars, and let the waves lap our skin and cleanse away the salt.

It was during this month I first began the healing process from the loss of my mother. It was after graduating college, after being discharged as a Peace Corps Volunteer in Bangladesh, and after teaching English in China. It was after seeing a psychiatrist and a psychologist for depression and dutifully going through the steps prescribed for health. It was the first time I began to recognize the trauma I'd been carrying around inside as an exploration to be investigated, a chance to wash the view from where my experiencing was being internalized.

Shortly after returning home, Eric and I began the process of trying to conceive. The years that followed held all of the joys and hurt and frustration one might imagine when it seems a life's purpose isn't being fulfilled. We miscarried at the end of the first year which became a blessing because we knew we could get pregnant. From there, it was simply trying to figure out why I couldn't stay pregnant. Years of tests and procedures and blood work and a surgery to turn the heart-shaped uterus I was born with into a triangle. Time to think about becoming the person I'd want my child to have as a parent. I travelled through SouthEast Asia. I enrolled and completed graduate studies in Creative Writing, and after ten years earned the designation of a Certified Yoga Therapist. Eric and I both established ourselves into careers that fed our minds and souls. And considered very rationally that perhaps our lot in life was not to raise a child, not to be parents in the traditional form, but rather some other yet unknown adventure awaited. I would birth books; and Eric would produce photographs. We'd create in other ways. We'd help others with our work in Brain Injury Medicine to move through tragedy and help guide in their own healing processes. We were conscious about being in a life of fulfillment and presence.

*

There are more stars in the sky than grains of sand on Earth : 100 billion galaxies each with an average of 100 billion stars. Clouds of gas and dust move chaotically, without form, gravity gathers more dust and gas towards the center, a random point positioning. Hydrogen and gravity begin to dance, spinning into heat, becoming energy, becoming light—fusing, they find stability for millions or billions of years. Eventually, hydrogen becomes helium and from fusion the star moves towards contraction, gathering into a singular flattened disc that spins in unison with the star's equator. This disc will give birth to all of the planets who orbit the star, creating worlds seemingly different from one another in appearance and personality. But born from the same dust—they are of the same essence.

One belief is before anything there was Chaos. An existence of disorder, mayhem, no form. Chaos made love to Night and their offspring produced all of the gods and all of man. Chaos and Night—that of no form mating with that of no light to create beings of form moving towards light. And these beings of form and light began to investigate and wonder and gaze at the stars. The Navajo name the coyote as prince of Chaos—the transformer, the catalyst. The stars were laid precisely in place and Coyote stole them and flung them across space to land randomly in the sky. The night our son was conceived, almost nine years to the day after our first conception, we were stopped in the road by a coyote, majestic in stance, the full moon lighting the street, highlighting his well-fed body. We were in Old Town Albuquerque at midnight, looking for the small cottage we'd rented for a friend's wedding. The road split and there was the coyote. Under the full moon, reflecting back the light of our existence, Chaos come to form.

We see the backbone first. A comma holding all that he will grow into, the pause we have been waiting for. Over the next seven months we watch him grow via sound waves, the ladder of bone, rungs of entropy, giving way to flippers and then arms and legs, hands and feet. We marvel at the dark spots containing his eyes and ears - the organs, the heart. The cord pulsing in communion between our bodies, floating inside the creation of us. I felt like I should be anxious, but there was a peace in the timing. A peace found from the guidance of the stars and the universe : the Cosmos : all that ever has been and all that ever will be. An acceptance. The !Kung Bushman of the Kalahari Desert in Botswana believe the milky way to be the backbone of the sky, illuminating the darkness—supporting the curvature of the universe.

I do worry I will be taken from this Earth before I'm ready. That my child will not know me. That I will not know him. And for that I write. I write because my mother wrote and because of that I have glimpses into her thinking, how she perceived the world. I have some of the whys to her hows. My youngest brother was six years old when she died. Recently he called me on what would have been her sixty-eighth birthday, balling, sobbing, at his realization that he did not know who his mother was. *We have her poetry* was all I could say. The essence of who she was poured into line and meter, tone and thought, early morning devotions under a not-yet-lit sky, guiding us from somewhere beyond. But still, he cries. And I cry. I cry randomly for her. For me. For my child who she will never meet. My heart is broken open and it floods to the core. The waves of knowing lapping with the waves of not knowing. I want to be good for him. I want to be clean for him. I want to feel. I want to feel again. I want to feel again and again and again.

From formless to form to formless once more. This being human is a cycle of creation at play. A cycle from nothing to something to nothing once more. From star dust and ether to mass of bones and blood and flesh. Organs that pump and feel and breathe. A body that encompasses. A mind that thinks. A soul who searches. And then back to dust, into the ether, a remembrance towards light. The vastness is enough to cause simultaneous heart and brain awe. Does it exist if we can't talk about it? How do we put into words the expanse of the universe? The immense space and time that exists beyond our sky? The space beyond the spin of Pluto. The information that we are but one sun in a plethora of suns more numerous than the sands of our beaches? And if this one fact isn't enough to blow the mind open, what of the possibility of other worlds with life? And if there isn't, our world becomes even more miraculous, that we might exist out of chance or divine insight or grit? It's enough to make us stop. No matter what your spiritual belief, but especially if you believe in a God, this Earth is precious. A gift. An offering of what can be and what is and who we are. Our essence come to light.

I watch him sleep, his mass growing, expanding. The neurons in his brain fusing and becoming rays of knowledge. Rumi, you are the most precious element in our life. I cannot predict the world or the actions of others or any of the possibility ahead, but I can, with my whole being, say we will love you. We will give you the tools to become a contributing citizen and an honorable human. We want Joy for you. We want Love for you. We want you to find awe, to be in openness, and to exist in presence, while you are here on this earth in this form.

THIS IS THE END OF THE LINE

Horse, the white hulk of it invades our reason—
    the strangeness of form seen from down the beach
    and in failing light—
    but as we draw near the eerie becomes concrete.
    Just a shell of what held once
    a life gone green and galloping;
    a pit as dark as mystery itself
    gone empty of sight and blinking.

Life,
    given over to a pile of stale hay
    balanced over a grave begun—
    not finished, rain-spoiled maybe.

And we,
    inhabitants of this dark world
    where trees stand sentinel and gray of leaves
    walk hurriedly upwind to pass quickly
    but signs of death,
    of shells empty of all inhabitant,
    map our path, crush fragile beneath our feet.

And I
    want you I want you to inhabit
    the beaches of my understandings,
    to gallop along this late winter terrain,
    stringing shells along long trains
    of my footsteps left solitary
    in the red mud stillness of the Brazos.

Adleman, Nancy Buquoi. "An Insufficiency of Jackson Square." 1969. "A Pilgrim Piece." 1971. "Cartwheel: Sunday P.M. Before Monday A.M." 1986. "Circles." 1978. "Dialect of the Heart." 1992. "Departure." 1992. "Dune Visitor." 1992. "Exchange." 1991. "Fields." 1969. "Flood Form." 1969. "Flying Without Nets: V" 1991. "Impending Storm." 1968. "On Traveling Great Distances." 1968. "Passage." 1991. "Process." 1969. "Sojourn." 1991. "The Mute Procession." 1969. "This is the End of the Line." 1974. "This Marriage." 1974. "Traiku." 1967. "We'd Get No Further." 1971. "Wellspring." 1992.

Alighieri, Dante. *The Inferno.* Trans. John Ciardi. New York: Signet Classics, 2009.

Amtrak. *Lake Shore Limited.* 8 October 2015. *Texas Eagle/Sunset Limited.* 9-11 October 2015. *California Zephyr.* 2-3 February 2016. *Empire Builder.* 4-6 February 2016. *Coast Starlight.* 7-8 February 2016. *California Zephyr.* 8-9 February 2016.

Ball, Jr., Don. *Portrait of the Rails: From Steam to Diesel.* New York: Galahad Books, 1972.

Barks, Coleman and John Moyne. *The Essential Rumi.* New Jersey: Castle Books, 1997.

Barks, Coleman and Michael Green. *The Illuminated Prayer: The Five-Times Prayer of The Sufis.* New York: Ballantine Books-Random House, 2000.

Beccaria, Cesare. *Of Crimes and Punishments and Other Writings.* 1764. Trans. Aaron Thomas and Jeremy Parzen. Toronto: The University of Toronto Press, 2008.

"Black Reaction—La Reazione nera." *Nobelprize.org.* Nobel Media AB 2014.

Boehle, Richard. "Telegraph Enables More Flexible Train

Order Operation." RailsWest.com. 07 Nov 2016.

Caplan, Lincoln. "Richard Glossip and The End of The Death Penalty." *The NewYorker.* 30 Sept 2015.

Coates, Ta-Nehisi. "The Black Family in the Age of Mass Incarceration." *The Atlantic.* Oct 2015

Cunningham, W. and P.D. Zelazo. "Attitudes and Evaluations: A Social Cognitive Neuroscience Perspective." *Trends in Cognitive Sciences.* 2007.
11:97-104.

Death Penalty Information Center. *Deathpenaltyinfo.org*

Didion, Joan. "Self-Respect: It's Source, It's Power." *Vogue.* 1 Aug 1961. 62-63.

Dieter, Richard. "Millions Misspent: What Politicians Don't Say About the High Costs of the Death Penalty." *The Death Penalty Information Center.* Oct 1992. Rev. 1994.

"DNA Exonerations Nationwide." *The Innocence Project.* 17 March 2016. *Innocenceproject.org*

Dobzhansky, Theodosius. "Nothing in Biology Makes Sense Except in the Light of Evolution." *The American Biology Teacher* 35. (March 1973) 125-129.

Ecenbarger, W. "Perfecting Death: When the State Kills it Must Do So Humanely. Is That Possible?" *The Philadelphia Inquirer Magazine* 23 January 1994.

Emerson, Ralph Waldo. "Experience." *Self-Reliance and Other Essays.* New York: Dover Thrift Editions, 1993.

"Faces of Death Row." 12 October 2018.

"Facts About the Death Penalty." *Deathpenaltyinfo.org.* 12

May 2016. 11 April 2018. 5 March 2019.

Foucault, Michel. "Discipline & Punish." Trans. Alan Sheridan. New York: Vintage-Random House, 1977.

Frankyl, Viktor. *Man's Search for Meaning.* 1959. Boston: Beacon Press, 2006. Freud, Sigmund. *Project for a Scientific Psychology.* 1895.

Furman v. Georgia, 408 US 238 (1972).

Future Islands. *Singles.* 4AD, 2014.

Garden State. Dir. Zach Graff. Perf. Zach Graff, Peter Sars-gaard, Natalie Portman. Fox Searchlight Pictures, 2004.

Gregg v. Georgia, 428 US 153 (1976).

Halper, Katie. "Clayton 'Rape Victims Should Relax and Enjoy It,' Williams is Funding TX GovGOP nominee Greg Abbott." *RawStory.com 08 Oct 2014.*

Harrison, Karen and Anouska Tamony. "Death Row Phenomenon, Death Row Syndrome and Their Affect on capital Cases in the US." *Internet Journal of Criminology.* 2010.

Hawking, Stephen. "The Universe in a Nutshell." New York, Bantam: 2001.

Hillman, Harold. "The Possible Pain Experienced During Executions by Different Methods." *Perception* 22.6 (1993): 745-753.

Hoover, Herbert. "Radio Address to the Nation on Unemployment Relief." October 18, 1931. Online by Gerhard Peters and John T. Woolley, *The American Presidency Project.*

"Houston History." *TexasBest.com.*

Hume, David. *An Enquiry Concerning Human Understanding.* 1748. Indianapolis: Hackett Publishing Company, 1977.

Kahneman, Daniel. *Thinking Fast and Slow.* New York: Farrar, Straus and Giroux, 2011.

Kandel, Eric R. *In Search of Memory: The Emergence of a New Science of Mind.* New York: W. W. Norton & Company, 2006.

King, Jr., Martin Luther. "Christmas Eve Sermon." 24 Dec 1967, Ebenezer Baptist Church, Atlanta, GA.

Kübler-Ross, Elisabeth. *On Death and Dying: What the Dying Have to Teach Doctors, Nurses, Clergy & Their Own Families.* New York: Scribner, 1969.

Loggins, Kenny. "Danny's Song." 1970.

McKnight, Ann. Phone Conversation. 26 August 2015.

Milgram, Rabbi Goldie. *Meaning & Mitzvah: Daily Practices for Reclaiming Judaism Through Prayer, God, Torah, Hebrew, Mitzvoth and Peoplehood.* Vermont: Jewish Lights Publishing, 2005.

Modest Mouse. *Good News for People Who Like Bad News.* Epic/Sony, 2004.

"My Little Hundred Million." *Revisionist History* from Malcolm Gladwell and Panoply Media, Season 1, Episode 6, *Revisionisthistory.com.*

Nelson, Maggie. "The Argonauts." Minneapolis: Graywolf Press, 2016. "Numbers 23:23." *Biblehub.com.*

Nietzsche, Friedrich. *Twilight of the Idols."* 1895. Trans. Walter Kaufmann and R.J. Hollingdale. *Handprint.com.*

Palmer, Chris. "The Neuron Doctrine, circa 1894." *The Scientist.* 1 November 2013.

Poole, Claire. "What Ever happened to Clayton Williams: Ten Years After He Ran for Governor, Oil's Well. So's Gas." *Texas Monthly.* June 1999.

Puentes, Robert, Adie Tomer, and Joseph Kane. "A New Alignment: Strengthening America's Commitment to passenger Rails." *Metropolitan Policy Program at Brookings.* March 2013.

Reznikoff, Iegor. "Sound Resonance in Prehistoric Times: A Study of Paleolithic Painted Caves and Rocks." *The Journal of Acoustical Society of America* 123.5 (2008): 4138-41.

Rickey, Gail. "Two Businesswomen go In-Cahoots to Sell Texas." *Houston Business Journal.* 30 September 1985.

Rossi, Pelegrino. *Traité de Droit Pénal.* Bruxelles: Société Belge de Librairie, 1841. Rushing, Josh. Interview with Michael Selsor. "Interview with a Death Row Inmate." *Aljazeera.* 10 May 2012.

"Sir William Henry Perkin." *Encyclopedia Brittanica. Encyclopædia Britannica Online. Encyclopædia Britannica Inc., 2016.*

Teachey, Lisa. "Jury Sends Man Back to Death Row in Slaying." *The Houston Chronicle.* 7 September 2002.

"Texas Court Cites Lawyer in Overturning Death Penalty." *The New York Times. 26* October 2000.

"Texas Death Row Prison Roster." *social.Prisonmatepenpal.com.* 9 April 2011.

The Compact Oxford English Dictionary. 2nd ed. New York: Oxford University Press, 1991.

Trop v. Dulles, 356 US 86 (1958).

Turner, Alan. "Supreme Court Won't Consider Houston Killer's Demand for Information About Execution Drug." *The Houston Chronicle* 9 June 2014.

Tzanakakis, Konstantinos. "The Railroad Track and Its Long Term Behavior." Berlin: Springer-Verlag Berlin Heidelberg, 2013.

"Uniform Correspondence Rules." *Texas Department of Criminal Justice.* BP-03.91 (rev. 3) 23 August 2013.

Veldt, John. Phone Conversations. 2015-2016.

Waits, Tom. "San Diego Serenade." *The Heart of Saturday Night.* Asylum Records, 1974.

"What is Life in Prison Without Parole?" *ProCon.org.* 22 August 2008.

Williams, Tennessee. *The Milk Train Doesn't Stop Here Anymore.* New York: Two Rivers Enterprises, Inc., 1963.

Wolmar, Christian. *The Great Railroad Revolution: The History of Trains in America.* New York: Public Affairs, 2012.

Young, Kevin. *The Art of Losing: Poems of Grief and Healing.* New York: Bloomsbury, 2010.

FOUND POEM

i take the summer inside me for a while   Nancy Buquoi Adleman
                                                 AN INSUFFICIENCY OF
                                                 JACKSON SQUARE

there is a field I'll meet you there   Mevlana Jelaluddin Rumi
                                                 OUT BEYOND IDEAS

i am not alone   Nancy Buquoi Adleman
                                                 TRAIKU

my feet are planted as one who stands waiting   Nancy Buquoi Adleman
                                                 IMPENDING STORM

actions become the love itself   Nancy Buquoi Adleman
                                                 THIS MARRIAGE

where is the wonder?   Nancy Buquoi Adleman
                                                 ON TRAVELING GREAT
                                                 DISTANCES

she asked me to teach her how   Nancy Buquoi Adleman
                                                 CARTWHEEL: SUNDAY P.M.
                                                 BEFORE MONDAY A.M.

important, life-serving experiences are learned Eric Kandel
                                                 IN SEARCH OF MEMORY

and tell me everything is going to be all right Kenny Loggins
                                                 DANNY'S SONG

somewhere there must be buoyancy   Nancy Buquoi Adleman
                                                 WE'D GET NO FURTHER

all of me that belonged to you.
i will become tomorrow   Nancy Buquoi Adleman
                                                 FIELDS

abandon all hope   Dante Alighieri
                                                 THE INFERNO

an hour comes and opens me into the dark   Nancy Buquoi Adleman
                                                 PROCESS

spin me long as silver thread.
hold me heavy against a spring dusk   Nancy Buquoi Adleman
                                                 CIRCLES

a strange new fossil—   Nancy Buquoi Adleman
                                                 EXCHANGE

the steady, granular accumulation
of the dripping, dripping of inner springs   Nancy Buquoi Adleman
PASSAGE

my blood pulses a prayer   Nancy Buquoi Adleman
DUNE VISITOR

i must speak a language i never knew i knew   Nancy Buquoi Adleman
DIALECT OF THE HEART

at least partially for the loss   Eric Kandel
IN SEARCH OF MEMORY

i wing my way on the echoes   Nancy Buquoi Adleman
DEPARTURE

the upheaved roots, the jumble of rock,
a weathered feel of smooth bark   Nancy Buquoi Adleman
SOJOURN

it is the consistency of things slipping
into pallor that brings me to this field   Nancy Buquoi Adleman
THE MUTE PROCESSION

hollowed out of heaven
stars point their light towards my eyes   Nancy Buquoi Adleman
FLYING WITHOUT NETS

of some things, what we know
that can be seen is enough   Nancy Buquoi Adleman
WELLSPRING

poetry is here with us   Nancy Buquoi Adleman
A PILGRIM PIECE

stringing shells along the trains   Nancy Buquoi Adleman
of my footsteps left solitary   THIS IS THE END OF THE
in the red mud stillness of the Brazos   LINE

Sarah Abigail Adleman, circa 1983